Proactive Media Relations

Proactive Media Relations
A Canadian Perspective

Third Edition

Mark Hunter LaVigne

CENTENNIAL
COLLEGE

Centennial College Press
Toronto

Centennial College Press
951 Carlaw Avenue
Toronto, Ontario M4K 3M2
https://centennialcollegepress.com/

Previous editions of this book were published under the title *Making Ink and Airtime.*

ISBN-13: 978-0-919852-74-7 (text)
ISBN-13: 978-0-919852-75-4 (trade)

This book is dedicated to my professional family,
the Canadian Public Relations Society

Contents

Foreword
William Wray Carney

The Canadian news media and their global colleagues carry a great deal of responsibility and immense power to stimulate positive change in society. The media relations practice must rise to the challenges of providing the news media with legitimate information, in the format most suited to them, in order to assist with and expedite that process.... It is when we are knowledgeable, aware and engaged that communicators are at our best.

—*Michael Nowlan, former president and CEO, Marketwired*

Mr. Nowlan's comments on the state of media and media relations continue to be relevant. This new edition of *Proactive Media Relations: A Canadian Perspective* has been revised and updated to reflect the changing nature of media and media relations in this country today. Technological change, changes in media ownership and direction, and the advent of new digital media are all occurring quickly and unpredictably, making it all the more important that practitioners keep up with change and be able to use the new tools to the best advantage of their clients.

Proactive Media Relations covers the basics of the media relations practice, and nicely balances traditional media relations (the news conference and news release for television, newspapers and radio) and working with digital and social media to get the message out in more channels. Regardless of whether you're working with traditional or newer media, the main elements of media relations remain the same: Define your market as narrowly as possible, determine the means of communications by which they receive information, craft messages that resonate with your target audience, send them out through the appropriate media channels, and engage your audience. Unlike other means of communications, media relations relies on an independent third party—reporters, editors and producers—to get the message out, and Mark LaVigne rightfully focuses on building and maintaining the reporter/media relations relationship.

Because I respect Mark's work experience, I asked him to join fellow colleague Colin Babuik and me as co-authors of *In the News: The Practice of Media Relations in Canada* (University of Alberta Press, third edition, 2019). Practitioners are advised to have copies of both texts. The strengths of this book are its corporate and national focus and its extensive case studies. *Proactive Media Relations* is a quick read and will be of use to the first-time practitioner trying to work effectively with the media, as well as for veterans who need a handy reference. Students and teachers will also find it of value.

Like many practitioners of media relations, Mark has worked in both media and public relations. He worked as a journalist in Edmonton, Calgary and Toronto, giving him a national perspective, and has a Master of Arts in Journalism from the University of Western Ontario. He has worked in public relations for 25 years in a Toronto-based practice. He teaches as well as practises.

Introduction
Daniel Granger

I have known Mark LaVigne for more than 20 years and have had the opportunity to collaborate with him on dozens of mandates with a variety of clients: businesses but also NPOs. Mark is a great PR professional with strong personal values whose work ethic is exemplary. But it is in his particular field of expertise, media relations, which he excels. He practised journalism for several years and he is very familiar with the workings of these organizations and the constraints and demands of the media on journalists. He has retained great respect for the work of journalists and has developed lasting professional friendships with many of them in several parts of the country.

Although he made the transition to the world of public relations before the explosion of the web, he continued his interest in journalism and closely watched the increasing impact of new media technologies on the work of journalists. Over the last twenty years, he has successfully piloted countless media relations campaigns because he knows and understands the work of journalists and because he respects their role. Always focused on rigor and honesty, he knows in detail all the elements that must be gathered to create "news," to attract the interest of specific journalists depending on their media and their target audience.

Mark's book is an outstanding collection of good practices, a real toolbox, to allow young PR practitioners as well as those who are more experienced to work efficiently, intelligently and respectfully with journalists. We live in an environment where the media have been in a deep crisis for almost three decades. The number of people employed in the media has decreased considerably. But their work remains essential to allow healthy communication and the open and balanced debates that lead to progress and ensure the quality of our democratic societies and institutions.

Despite the impact of the technological revolution that has, among other things, spawned the birth and explosion of social media that have become essential communications tools, Mark remains deeply convinced of the importance of journalism and of the essential role of the PR professional to meet their needs and interest.

As a concrete example, Mark was involved for almost two years in promoting the Jesuit Canadian Canoe Pilgrimage 2017, a project of the Jesuits in English Canada that aimed to promote reconciliation between the Indigenous, French and English peoples of Canada. From July 20 to August 15, 2017, the paddlers of the Jesuit Collaborators travelled from the shores of Georgian Bay to the shores of the Island of Montreal. During the two years prior to departure, Mark developed and implemented a media relations plan to promote and communicate at every step of the way during the event. The media coverage of this event was an enormous and complex challenge that Mark managed carefully, making it an outstanding success and one that would have been difficult to achieve using only social media.

Through his professional experience, publications and academic roles at several colleges offering public relations programs, Mark makes a remarkable contribution to the promotion and development of the public relations profession in Canada. On behalf of CPRS and all our members, I am deeply grateful to him.

Proactive Media Relations

What is Public Relations and Where Does Media Relations Fit?

Public relations (often referred to as "PR"), the 100-or-so-year-old multidiscipline, can be described as the hub of the communications wheel for any organization, whether non-profit, for profit, government or non-government.

Running out from that hub are a number of spokes (communications lines) that provide a two-way flow of information between an organization and its numerous stakeholders.

While most business people are familiar with advertising (the granddaddy of marketing communications), public relations remains relatively misunderstood. Therefore, many of those responsible for initiating or procuring public relations services do not fully understand the power of public relations and what it can accomplish for them.

PR is the two-way communications that takes place between an organization and its numerous "publics" or audiences, both internal and external. Hence, it is far more than just publicity in the sense of generating ink or airtime for a celebrity or, in the political arena, the "spin doctoring" that's done to attempt to convert bad press into good.

PR is proactive and positive, always trying to avoid a problem before it occurs. Those who do not understand PR think it exists only to clean up problems or do damage control. That is an incomplete view of public relations, which uses relationship building as one of its essential tactics. Effective PR builds strong teams, often driving those teams to consensus.

There are several disciplines within PR, including media relations, investor relations, government relations, community relations and employee (internal) relations, to name just a few.

As PR matures, it has become more integrated with the traditional marketing communications disciplines of advertising and sales promotion. Some people claim that it is now becoming the strategic engine for these disciplines, especially as marketing communications budgets have become more evenly shared among disciplines in the past few years.

Although some argue that advertising is dead and PR is rising from its ashes, public relations is most effective when it's integrated with other marketing communications disciplines. Frankly, a PR-friendly organization will apply its strong PR thinking to every level of the organization, from front-door reception to back-door shipping and receiving.

Media relations is one of PR's main disciplines, and arguably one of the most difficult. It is one of the only marketing communications disciplines that must go through a gatekeeper to reach the end audience. The media relations strategy that enables key messaging to pass through the gatekeeper intact is easily applied to other marketing communications disciplines. Finding the "newsworthiness" in a message necessarily removes non-essential information. It intellectually focuses organizations to get down to "brass tacks."

Media relations can be very effective when key messaging is adopted by advertising and sales promotions (such as point-of-purchase) and rolled out in an integrated manner. Key messaging can also be adopted by other divisions of a company, from sales to human resources, and once again, from the reception desk to shipping and receiving.

PR practitioners should be the guardians of an organization's brand, and that concept of brand is not just reserved for a private sector, product-oriented company. The concept of brand—what an organization is, what it is about, what it wants to say—is the organization's being, and public relations is often its protector and conscience.

PR is also about truth. Journalists, like police officers, develop an instinct for truth. Non-truthful messaging certainly won't get through the journalistic gatekeeper very often, and if it does and is found out, an organization will find itself in deep trouble. Truth is an essential tool in the public relations arsenal. Canada's professional PR organizations, such as the Canadian Public Relations Society (CPRS), have adopted strict codes of ethics to ensure practitioners continue to guard their organizational brands with integrity.

Professional organizations in the field of public relations have also doggedly pursued accreditation programs to teach, test and recognize senior practitioners. As the profession matures, so does that process. The profession is multifaceted, vibrant, and filled with many dedicated professionals who are directly involved in many facets of modern society.

The Canadian Public Relations Society uses a concise definition of public relations that has been duly recognized by the Global Alliance, the international association of PR associations, and which is worth repeating here: "Public relations is the strategic management of relationships between an organization and its diverse publics, through the use of communication, to achieve mutual understanding, realize organizational goals and serve the public interest."[1]

1. Flynn, T., Gregory, F., & Valin, J. (2008). CPRS public relations definition. Retrieved from http://www.cprs.ca/about/who-we-are.

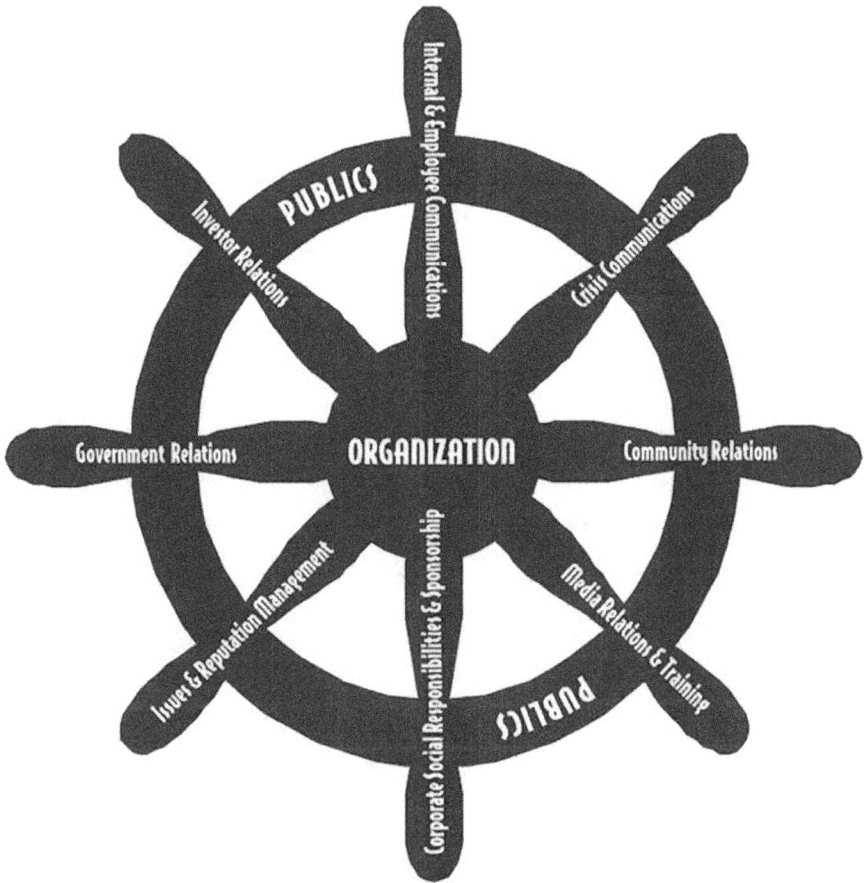

The PR Wheel

It's a PESO World Now for the Average Practitioner

Although this book focuses on the *earned* aspect of public relations, where we offer or broker viable information to the traditional news media at no cost on either side of the equation, more and more the PR practitioner simultaneously deals with other aspects of the *PESO formula*: *paid*, *earned*, *shared*, and *owned*.

In the earned category, that transfer of information can also include bloggers and influencers, and likewise in the realm of investor relations as well. But the moment it involves "payment" to secure that coverage, then it becomes *paid*. We mention this in other parts of the book and the ethics surrounding it, but when it becomes paid, it should be indicated so, with a variety of descriptors such as "sponsored content."

A media relations practitioner may also communicate with news media via social media, and younger journalists may only communicate this way. But the transfer of information through these information channels—from Facebook to Instagram—falls into the realm of *shared*.

A media relations practitioner will also quite likely transfer news releases into short or feature articles, offered into several channels, including the client's website, newsletter, corporate magazine, even brochures. This is *owned*.

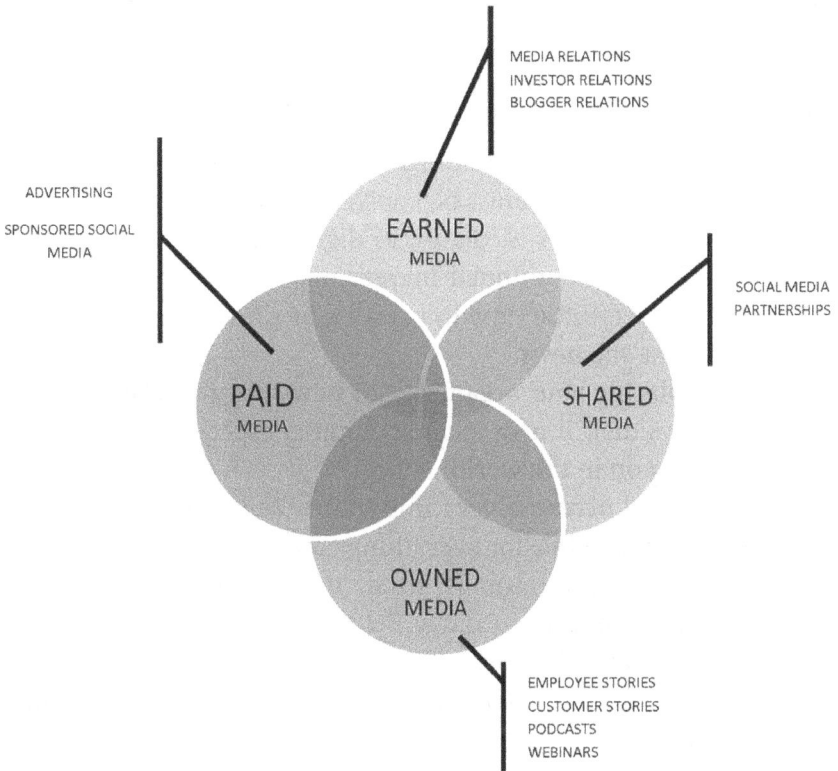

MEDIA RELATIONS
INVESTOR RELATIONS
BLOGGER RELATIONS

ADVERTISING

SPONSORED SOCIAL
MEDIA

EARNED
MEDIA

SOCIAL MEDIA
PARTNERSHIPS

PAID
MEDIA

SHARED
MEDIA

OWNED
MEDIA

EMPLOYEE STORIES
CUSTOMER STORIES
PODCASTS
WEBINARS

The PESO model was introduced by Gini Dietrich in her book *Spin Sucks* (2014). The model emphasizes the importance of the sector where the four types of media overlap.

Media Relations Practice

After working for decades as a media relations consultant and for five years as a journalist, I've come to the conclusion that five basic parameters govern successful media relations. They are:

- Content
- Context
- Organizational access
- Proactive response
- Relationships with the news media

Content must be tightly written, with a focus on the facts and an avoidance of hyperbole. It must be constructed in an electronic format and delivered to the news media on a "digital platter." The inundation journalists suffer, plus continued merger mania in the news business, means they have very little time to research or sift through (useless) information to mine the news.

Context is placing your organization's news within the ebb and flow of the daily news diet. It also includes timing, especially in relation to what else is going on in the world.

Organizational access is very important. The news media operate on a much tighter schedule for everything compared to regular business responsiveness. A radio journalist needs the information or interview requested that hour, not the next day. Television needs it the by the same afternoon, at the latest. And print by mid-afternoon!

Proactive response is essential in creating a two-way flow of information between the organization and news media. The more proactive an organization is over time, the less severe the reaction by the media if there's a crisis. If the news media know your organization as open and honest through years of access, then the worst part of a crisis (what are they hiding?) may be mitigated or at least minimized.

Relationships with the news media go hand-in-hand with access. Over time, if your organization and PR practitioners have been open and honest with the media, that access and honesty go a long way in raising your organization's credibility and its position on a journalist's priority list. If you serve their information needs, in the long term you will generate coverage on your behalf.

How Media Relations Helps the Marketing Plan

You're the product manager or marketing director responsible for marketing a new product—let's say a new high-tech device.

You have a limited budget to promote the new product, say $20,000, and you wonder what will give you the better bang for your buck, media relations or advertising?

Your strategic planning to date has definitely satisfied the "new, better, different" criteria, with an identifiable niche, clearly defined target audiences, and a strong point-of-difference from your competition. In short, your product offers strategic merit.

You wish you could do both media relations and advertising, and have seen the effectiveness of integrated campaigns that have ten times your current budget.

You have research data that clearly indicates which media your target audiences consume. You realize you can't even come close to getting enough repetition on the broadcast segments highlighted, and that even purchasing print advertising at the frequency and scale you think is needed may be quite difficult.

So what value can media relations bring to the table?

First of all, a seasoned media relations practitioner will help you see the product from the news media's point of view. Your strategic thinking should be focused in the direction of what an editor and/or freelance journalist will see. In short, where is the real story? In what context does it fit? What does your product offer their audience? Development of this kind of strategic key messaging is imperative to give your product's key messaging a chance to get through the journalistic gatekeeper to the desired end audience, your ultimate target.

Media relations is one of the few marketing communications disciplines that has to go through such a gatekeeper exclusively. But in that fact lies its true value. Because the gatekeeper is charged with the formidable task of informing his or her audience with third-party, relatively unbiased information, that information is considered far more believable by an audience than an advertisement. And as the pace of technology development explodes logarithmically, journalists realize the value of helping their audiences make crucial technology acquisition decisions. In many ways, the opinion of the journalist is like that of a trusted family member, neighbour or friend.

The ultimate goal of good marketing communications is generating favourable word-of-mouth advertising through product trial. Good media coverage is just that: word-of-mouth from a trusted source, comparable to a family member, neighbour or friend who has tried the product and says it's good. So make the media an integral (if not primary) part of the product trial/word-of-mouth advertising process. Just make sure to provide an adequate supply of the new product for news media demos.

Many marketers equate news media coverage with what it would cost to fill a similar amount of airtime or space with an advertisement. It is very important to remember that one cannot buy editorial coverage. It's not for sale. For that reason, its believability with an audience is far greater than the content of an ad. How many times more believable requires a lot more space than we have available here to address properly, and frankly, a lot more work by the PR industry to develop academically endorsed, empirical paradigms to determine the true value of an impression. Just remember, media relations, unlike advertising, is more than counting impressions, it's a major step in building long-term relationships with the gatekeepers who control access to your target audiences.

The State of the News Media and the "News Hole"

One of the first rules of media relations is to know the media. When you know something about the environment in which journalists have to work, you appreciate their deadlines and their perspectives, all of which helps to improve your skill in reaching them with your story or news release.

During the past decades, the news media, particularly private-sector newspapers, magazines, radio and television outlets, have suffered from the same economic turmoil as many other private-sector organizations. Globalization, recession, national and multinational mergers, and technological revolutions have significantly affected the business side of the news media, causing upheaval in newsrooms across the country.

Computers and computer networks have enabled news reporting functions to be performed by far fewer people than a decade or two ago, while the same technology has exponentially increased the amount of news available for dissemination. Consequently, there is more news to be processed by fewer people. CBC's Ira Basen, among others, has been tracking these trends.

Furthermore, a dramatic shift in advertising revenues from mass advertising to much more targeted online marketing has drastically reduced the advertising revenues available to the majority of private-sector mass news outlets. The consequence for anyone submitting a news story or media release? The "news hole" (the space in which proactive news can be placed) has dramatically shrunk.

Other trends include a change in the demographics of reporters and editors. Many journalists—those who survived recessions, mergers and technological downsizing—have stayed in their positions longer. The rate of turnover in the news business traditionally is high, but in major news markets such as Toronto there is far less movement than ever before, partly because fewer jobs are available. It still takes the average journalist ten years to get promoted into major markets. But once they arrive, economic conditions keep those reporters in their same jobs, rather than moving up into other editorial positions. Because of these factors, journalists are older, smarter, generally better educated, and usually more cynical than their predecessors. Cynicism often breeds distrust, making the current generation of news reporters more suspicious and more formidable than ever.

In a quest for greater audience numbers, and to attract dwindling advertising dollars, "tabloid" journalism has risen in popularity. Tabloid journalism tends to be sensationalistic, unbalanced and controversial. It has spread from supermarket tabloids like the *National Enquirer* to television and is anticipated to eventually infect radio news and more serious daily broadsheets.

Specific Inundation Examples

- Marc Saltzman, one of Canada's most successful technology freelancers, receives more than 300 emails a day.
- In a 2005 survey, Ipsos Reid found that 61 per cent of business journalists prefer email for communication, compared to 18 per cent preferring phone calls and 6 per cent faxes. As well, 28 per cent stated bluntly that phone is *not* the way they want to be approached.

The Canadian News Marketplace: A Quick Snapshot

- Concentration of ownership
- Gridlock on the electronic superhighway
- According to Ipsos Reid, business journalists receive 150 news releases a week, of which 18 per cent are used; 19 news conference invitations a month, of which half get assigned to a reporter; 60 annual reports a year, of which only 16 per cent are used quickly; and 20 media kits a month, of which 19 per cent are used.

The News Fence

A "news fence" has always existed between advertising and editorial (the news gatherers) in most news media organizations. Journalists are trained to literally bite the hand that feeds them, that is, to be distrustful of the very advertisers who ultimately pay at least some part of their salaries. In public broadcasting, this relationship is even more antagonistic.

Public broadcasters, such as TV Ontario (TVO), generally do not rely on advertising (CBC Television is an exception) for the bulk of their revenue and therefore have an even more entrenched anti-private-sector bias than their private-sector media counterparts. Some of the programs most critical of private-sector organizations are broadcast on public networks. The economic and demographic forces influencing private-sector news media that were described earlier are even more profound in this media sector. Government cutbacks have turned public broadcasting on its ear, and will likely continue to do so for years to come.

In smaller private-sector media outlets, such as some trade magazines or broadcast outlets, the "news fence" is thinner than in major markets. But in bigger or more established media outlets, the fence can be as thick as a bomb-shelter wall.

Nonetheless, private-sector proactive media relations (for example, a product launch) is often suspected by many in the news media as "veiled advertising." A common media response is: "if you want to buy advertising, you should go down the hall." In reactive situations, the media generally suspect private-sector representatives are "lying" or trying to hide something. You are considered guilty until proven innocent in the court of media opinion.

You may ask yourself: "Why should I even bother? Why not say 'no comment' until they go away?"

The answer is simple. They won't go away and you will be tried in the court of media opinion in absentia. Furthermore, you will be missing a significant opportunity—an opportunity to defend yourself properly, to set the record straight, and to get positive messages about your organization on the public record.

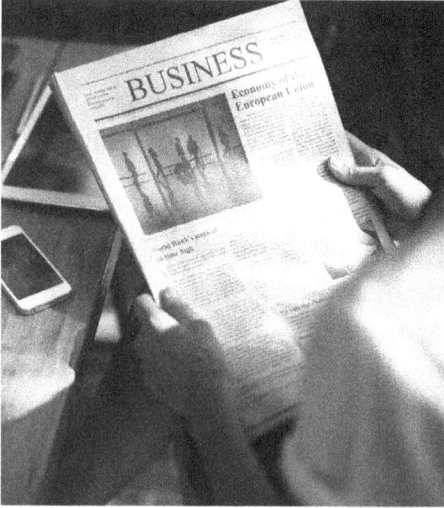

Proactive and Reactive Media Relations

There are generally two types of media opportunities: proactive and reactive media relations.

Proactive media relations generally involves going to the media proactively, usually for positive stories, but sometimes for negative ones as well. Reasons for such contact run the full gamut of proactive communications, including new product or service launches, product re-launches, appointment announcements, mergers, as a part of larger lobbying efforts, and even reorganizations.

Methods of media contact can include news releases and social-media news releases, special events, news conferences, video and audio news releases, media tours, and telephone or personal meetings with journalists with whom you have developed professional or personal rapport.

You are in the driver's seat. You go to the media when you are ready, on your schedule, and generally following your agenda.

Reactive media relations generally involves the media coming to you, usually within a negative context, such as layoffs, product recalls, reorganizations, poor stock performance, specific industry regulatory issues, fires, and illegal activity within the organization. This kind of media relations is often called *crisis communications*. We like to call it *deliberate crisis response communications* because you should be ready to deal with these kinds of situations when they arise.

Newsworthiness

Within the realm of proactive media relations, a "newsworthiness checklist" has been developed to help determine whether or not a story you propose taking to the media yourself, or through a public relations practitioner, is newsworthy.

What Does "Newsworthy" Mean?

Reporters and editors are, essentially, storytellers. "Newsworthy" means "good story." There are general criteria for what constitutes news, which are discussed in the following pages. However, each media outlet's choice of news is affected by its understanding of what its audience wants.

What is News?

Out of all the activity happening everywhere, reporters and editors choose what is *news*. They decide what is worthy of the front page of the paper, the cover of a magazine, or should be one of the dozen or so stories that makes it onto a television newscast.

Their decisions are based, to a certain extent, on practical considerations. When a television station has video of a fire, for instance, that story is much more likely to get covered in the newscast than if the camera crew did not get to the blaze in time.

For any story to make the news anywhere, the media must believe it will affect the public's mind or heart because it possesses at least one of the seven criteria of news:

- Impact
- Proximity
- Timeliness
- Prominence
- Conflict
- Novelty
- Human interest

If none of those criteria is particularly prominent, what you have is information, not news.

What Does It Mean to Publicize?

Publicizing means selling the media on the newsworthiness of an idea. It results in positive media coverage generated by a public relations practitioner, rather than by people or actions outside an organization's control.

Often, but not always, a good public relations practitioner can try to create news out of information by finding ways to stress one of the news criteria. Sometimes, for instance, the information can be made more timely and prominent by linking it to several similar initiatives happening elsewhere (this is sometimes called "putting a spin" on a story).

A good public relations practitioner knows the media market, knows the kind of stories that radio, TV, and print are looking for, knows if a story is local or broader, knows the format in which specific media like to receive their information.

A few general rules: TV likes action, print likes detail, and radio is somewhere in between, depending on the outlet and show. Attendance at an event has nothing to do with coverage. News releases should be short and written in a simple, declarative style (preferably in the style of The Canadian Press, Canada's national news agency) to be most effective, and to avoid triggering the "snicker factor," where guffaws erupt in the receiving newsroom.

The strong positive benefit of seeking publicity is tempered by the attendant uncertainty: once you broach a subject with the media, there is no guarantee it will be covered at all; or, if covered, that the story will be favourable.

Yet, since reporters will do negative stories if they want to anyhow, when we have a good story to tell the publicity is almost always worth the gamble.

What's My Story? Why Should Anyone Care?

The acid test of whether information can be turned into a newsworthy story is to answer, in a sentence, each of those two questions.

Unless there is some angle involving at least one of the seven criteria that can be brought to the fore, forget it. Your information is not newsworthy. Wait until you have something that is newsworthy.

The most important thing any public relations practitioner can do with the media is to develop a good relationship with them. This also applies to organizations seeking publicity. What is important is that the media see your PR practitioner, and your organization, as a reliable source of news. Don't waste their time pretending boring information is news. Every day, they receive hundreds of news releases, voicemails and emails from public relations practitioners vying for a shrinking news hole. To compete, you need the goods.

Even if the media promise to come to your event or pick up your news release, they may not. Your story may get pre-empted by another that scores higher in newsworthiness. We know of some news directors or assignment editors who say "yes" to everything, who say they will attend a news event or pick up a news release when they have no intention of doing so, just to get rid of PR people as quickly as possible.

Once you have a good story, a lot of proactive media relations has to do with timing, and at times, luck. You, or your PR people, have no control over natural or other disasters, or other significant stories that may occur at any moment, and shrink that already small news hole even more.

Newsworthiness in a Reactive Sense

Many journalists consider negative news as more newsworthy than positive news, because positive news happens more often than negative news and therefore negative news is rarer and more noteworthy. For example, in some US cities murders are so common that, apart from the particularly gruesome ones, they rarely get daily news coverage.

Often the media focus on negative stories because they are ever watchful of trends. You will notice if you monitor news media closely that after a big disaster of some kind, the media will then report with heightened interest subsequent similar but minor disasters in an attempt to establish some kind of trend.

PIXABAY

The News Spotlight

We like to describe the media as a roving spotlight. The spotlight will fix on a subject for a while, go away and then come back.

If the news media spotlight focuses on an issue close to your organization's heart, be prepared. The media may come knocking at your door. Conversely, media coverage trends can be used to your advantage.

Often, national interest stories need input from involved stakeholders, whether that be for a news agency such as CP, or a national newspaper looking for local angles.

Media monitoring and research is very important if you're to stay on top of these media trends and follow the media spotlight. It is much better to invest the time and money in such media intelligence than to have your telephone ring one day with a national newspaper or radio network reporter on the other end asking some very tough questions.

Where Does News Come from, How Are News Decisions Made, and When Are They Made?

Journalists are un-chartered but (in general) socially responsible professionals. By "un-chartered," we mean there is no set of criteria to enter or practise the craft. There is no College of Journalists or Journalism Society of Upper Canada to license journalists. There is no equivalent to the bar exams. In fact, among journalists there is an entrenched attitude that any form of professional control would endanger freedom of the press. Because of this, journalism may never evolve beyond the "craft" level into a real profession.

Education levels among journalists range from graduate degrees (rare) to non-completion of high school (more common, especially among "old school" journalists). Canadian newsrooms are filled with home-grown talent, as well as expatriate journalists from primarily the United States and Britain.

News comes from a large number of sources: as mentioned earlier, technology plays a major role. Generally, news services range from paid newswires (where clients pay by the word to have their news releases transmitted electronically into news rooms across the country, or around the world) to news agencies such as The Canadian Press (which distributes news to member newspapers or broadcast outlets). Other news agencies around the world worthy of note include the Associated Press (US) and Agence France-Presse (France).

Most major-market newsrooms have access to all of these services.

News also comes from public relations practitioners in one form or another, either proactively or reactively. Some studies suggest that up to 75 per cent of the news carried in a daily newspaper, radio or television newscast has at least been through a public relations practitioner's hands, if not actually crafted by them.

News outlets also gather their own news, generated by a reporter or editor's "sources," or even by tips received from that outlet's readers or audience members. Media outlets also have numerous standard "beats," where reporters and editors cover everything from police headquarters to city hall, from the local legislature to specific industries.

Staff at most media outlets meet at least once a day to decide on what's to be covered during that day's "news run." Story meetings occur usually in the morning, with radio being the earliest (usually before 9 a.m.) and television the latest (often just before lunch). Radio is now considered primarily an early morning news medium (before 9 a.m.), television an evening one, with newspapers generally being read in between, although all media are also battling for online instantaneity. The "all-news" broadcast format also attracts audiences throughout the day.

Through story meetings, news assignments are assigned by editors to reporters. Reporters will often suggest stories; in our experience, those suggestions usually will be accepted or rejected within seconds, about the same time it takes a PR practitioner the time to "pitch" a prospective story to a journalist.

Deadlines rule the newsroom. For daily newspapers, deadlines fall during the evening before the publication date. *The Globe and Mail* generally "goes to bed" at 6 p.m. because it is transmitted by satellite to be printed nationwide. The *Toronto Star*'s deadline is 10 p.m., and the *National Post* (also distributed nationwide like the *Globe*) as early as 5 p.m. Radio and The Canadian Press have the tightest deadlines (often hourly), followed by television (before the noon, suppertime and late night newscasts) and print. However, with everything shifting online for all media, these print deadline rules are going out with the bath water!

Diverse Target Audiences and Their Media Habits

For both external and internal communicators, never before has there been such a diverse group of audiences to target messaging towards nor such a plethora of media channels to do so. Although the exact dates for various generational groups are sometimes disputed—for instance, were the last of the Baby Boomers born in 1964 or 1965?—nonetheless it's helpful to explore the media habits for some of the groups noted below:

- Baby Boomers (born 1946–1964): 9.6 million in Canada in 2017, 80 million in the U.S.
- Generation X (born 1965–1976): 2.8 million in Canada, 51 million in the U.S.
- Generation Y/Millennials (born 1977–1995): 9.1 million in Canada, 75 million in the U.S.
- Generation Z, iGen or Centennials (born 1996 and later): 7.3 million in Canada, 23 million in the U.S. (and growing rapidly)[2]

The Center for Generational Kinetics (CGK), based in Austin, Texas, has done a considerable amount of research on these different cohorts. CGK notes that someone born during the three years on either side of the beginning or end of a generation will likely share characteristics of the adjoining group. Of course, other factors also come into play, including age of parents, urban or rural location, education level, and economic status.

Although other sources identify 2000 as the cut-off date for Millennials, CGK argues this is incorrect since the defining moment for this generation was the terrorist attacks on September 11, 2001.

Three key trends shape generational groups: parenting, technology, and economics. For example, according to CGK, many Baby Boomers want things to be easier for their kids; this attitude in turn helped create and reinforce Millennials' sense of entitlement, something which of course is a hotly debated topic!

Millennials have become the largest generation in the North American workforce and the fastest growing generation of customers in the

2. Statistics Canada, "Generations in Canada." Retrieved from http://www12.statcan.gc.ca/census-recensement/2011/as-sa/98-311-x/98-311-x2011003_2-eng.cfm. Also see Center for Generational Kinetics, "Info about Generations." Retrieved from http://genhq.com/faq-info-about-generations/.

marketplace, and so they are getting lots of attention these days.

The newest generation, Gen Z, and Millennials do not share a defining moment. As noted, for Millennials that moment was 9/11, but Gen Z, born in 1996 and later, has only vague childhood memories (or none at all) of that day.

Marketing firm WJ Schroer has provided additional information on the different generations, although its demarcation dates differ from CGK's.[3]

Their research divides Baby Boomers into two groups, Boomers I and Boomers II (which they call Generation Jones), because of the 20-year gap between oldest and youngest members of the cohort. Boomers I experienced significant historical events such as the Kennedy and King assassinations, the civil rights movement, and the Vietnam War. Boomers II (or Generation Jones) missed all of that. But Generation Jones did have Watergate, economic struggles such as the oil embargo of 1979, AIDs, and suffered in the shadow of Boomers I, who had the best jobs, opportunities, housing, and so on—an experience Boomers II share with Gen X and even Gen Y to a certain extent.

Boomers II were the first to be exposed to personal computing, but not until their adult years.

Gen X, according to the company, is the "lost generation," the first generation of "latchkey" kids, exposed to daycare and divorce. This generation is highly skeptical, has the lowest voter participation, and is the best educated. They were also the first to grow up with the personal computer, albeit ones that were rather primitive in comparison to those used by later groups.

Gen Y, also known as Millennials or Echo Boomers, are the children of mostly Boomer II's and have become, as mentioned, a very large group, almost as large as the Boomers themselves. They are considered sophisticated, technology-wise and immune to most traditional marketing and sales pitches. They are more racially and ethnically diverse. They have great influence over family purchases, and, one can argue, communications trends, an area that needs more study. Boomers II have taken to new technology to be able to communicate with their kids, whether that be Skype, texting or social media.

Gen Z, growing up with the latest technology, is known as the "mobile generation." One must assume that terror, whether that be domestic,

3. WJ Schroer, "Generations X, Y, Z and the Others." Retrieved from http://socialmarketing.org/archives/generations-xy-z-and-the-others/.

international, cyber or even the experience of natural disasters, is this generation's pivotal historical influencer. Much more study of this group is needed.

A 2016 article in *Food in Canada* further divides Gen Z into two groups, Gen We and Gen Z, citing research from global communications firm Zeno Group. Exploring generational differences, the article cites Environics research indicating that Gen X has the highest annual household income in Canada at $102,000, compared to $71,000 for Millennials and $98,000 for Baby Boomers (some of whom are now retired). Other demographic data for Gen X include the fact that 74 per cent are employed full time and 65 per cent are living with children.[4]

The article also cites Ipsos Reid research that breaks down Baby Boomers into two groups, "back-end boomers" (aged 52 to 60 in the year 2017), who make up 16 per cent of the Canadian population, and "front-end boomers" (aged 61 to 69), who account for 11 per cent of the population.

There is another sub-generation worth noting, called Xennials, according to Australian website MamaMia.[5] These are older Millennials born on the cusp of Generation X and Y between 1977 and 1983 who grew up without video games but became digitally savvy as adults.

Research also suggests that Gen X spends more time on social media and consumes more media overall, spending nearly seven hours a week on social media, compared to Millennials, who spent an hour less. Baby Boomers, the data suggests, spend just four hours per week. Gen X also spends 32 hours per week toggling between all media, compared to 27 hours for Millennials and 20 hours for Boomers. Interestingly, the data (collected by research firm Neilsen) suggests women do this more than men. Twenty-five per cent of their time online is spent on social media, compared to 19 per cent for males.[6]

Further insight is provided by a recent Business2Community.com article that cites BuzzPlant data on generational media consumption:

4. Rebecca Harris, "Who's Eating What?" *Food in Canada*, June 2016. Retrieved from https://www.foodincanada.com/features/whos-eating-what/.

5. Ryan Girdusky, "Older millennials abandon 'millennial' term, don't want to be associated with snowflakes," *Red Alert Politics*, July 1, 2017. Retrieved from http://redalertpolitics.com/2017/07/01/old-millennials-abandon-millennial-term-dont-want-associated-snowflakes/.

6. Ana Veciana-Suarez, "Gen-Xers spend more time on social media than millennials, report shows," *Toronto Star*, February 2, 2017. Retrieved from https://www.thestar.com/life/health_wellness/2017/02/02/gen-xers-spend-more-time-on-social-media-pages-than-millennials-report-shows.html.

- Gen Z is abandoning Facebook; 25 per cent left it in 2014 alone.
- 32 per cent of US teens say Instagram is their favourite social media platform.
- 32 per cent of Gen Z would like brands to reach them by email.
- 87 per cent of Millennials use Facebook, and they have the highest average number of friends on the platform.
- 43 per cent of Millennials want brands to reach them by email.
- Millennials believe that user-generated content is 50 per cent more trustworthy and 25 per cent more memorable than branded content.
- While 48 per cent of Gen X have a Twitter account, less than half are active users.
- More than one in three Pinterest users are Gen Xers.
- 40 per cent of GenXers prefer viewing content online on laptops, and 25 per cent of online shoppers are from Gen X.
- 84 per cent of Baby Boomers have Facebook accounts, only slightly less than Millennials.
- 58 per cent of Boomers visit a company's website after encountering a brand on social media.
- 41 per cent of Boomers have Pinterest accounts.

Interestingly, there is a marked difference in the time of day that different generational groups consume online data, according to an analysis of online consumption habits by Fractl and Buzzstream.[7] Boomers prefer to consume content in the early to late morning period (between 5 a.m. and noon) while Millennials and Gen Xers prefer to access content between 8 pm and midnight.

There is also a generational split when it comes to devices, according to the study. Boomers prefer desktops and laptops, as do Gen Xers, while Millennials are the biggest users of mobile. Still, only about 25 per cent use mobile devices as their primary means of going online, while most still use desktops and laptops the majority of the time.

All generations rank blog articles as their favourite type of content, and all generations also agree that images, comments, and ebooks rank in the next three places. In fifth place, Millennials prefer audiobooks (and perhaps podcasts?) while GenXers prefer case studies and Boomers prefer reviews.

7. Amanda Walgrove, "Infographic: How Millennials, Gen Xers, and Boomers Consume Content Differently," *Contently*, May 19, 2015. Retrieved from https://contently.com/2015/05/19/infographic-how-millennials-gen-xers-and-boomers-consume-content-differently/.

About 60 per cent of each group uses Facebook to share content. The next most popular network is YouTube, but only ten per cent of survey respondents said they used YouTube to share content. Thereafter, Boomers use Google+ the most, Gen-Xers prefer Twitter, and Millennials prefer Instagram and Tumblr.

All generations consume both traditional and digital media in varying degrees throughout their day. While Millennials are more digitally inclined, they still rely on traditional media to stay informed.

Interestingly, at least one study conducted by German market research company GfK in 2015 showed that the gap between Boomers and Millennials in media consumption was not as wide as often thought:

- Boomers consumed an average of only 3.4 per cent more magazines than Millennials.
- Millennials spent only seven more hours online each week than their Boomer counterparts.
- When it comes to Internet behaviour, again, there were more similarities in consumption patterns than differences. For instance, 40 per cent of Boomers used Facebook regularly, compared to 48 per cent of Gen X and 51 per cent of Millennials.

Gen Z is the newest generation with emerging consumer power but research data remains sparse. According to an article on Business2Community.com that drew on findings by Google and Ipsos, this generation has little concept of what daily activity was like before smartphones, online shopping, and social media.[8] A CNN study revealed that some 13-year-olds check their social media accounts as much as 100 times per day.[9]

This generation prefers to keep their personal lives "private," unlike some earlier generations, with 56.4 per cent using Snapchat. Snapchat allows them to interact with brands they love on a personal level as well as shop online if they see an ad they like, but at the same time allows them to keep their sharing private. They also prefer to connect with people via text messages more than twice as much as interacting with peo-

8. Arik Hanson, "The Evolving Media Consumption Habits of Gen Z–and What They Mean for Communicators," *Business2Community*, November 25, 2016. Retrieved from https://www.business2community.com/trends-news/evolving-media-consumption-habits-gen-z-mean-communicators-01708850.

9. The program is archived, along with supplementary material, at https://www.cnn.com/specials/us/being13.

ple in person. In fact, nearly three in 10 teens say they text people who are physically with them at the time. While they have access to multiple devices, smartphones reign supreme and are the most used devices for 13- to 17-year-olds, with 53 per cent of them using their smartphones to make purchases. They watch 2½ times more online video than TV, with 71 per cent watching more than three hours of online video every day.

Further research is needed on how transgenerational connections (such as between a Boomer parent and a Millennial offspring) influence preferred communications methods.

The finding that blog articles are a preferred form of communication for all groups, with a limit of 300 words and images embedded, provides a hint to communicators about which tactics can reach across generations. Perhaps since this form of communication traditionally is written in standard news style, it may be more effective in bridging generational differences.

How do these generational differences impact multicultural Canada and the media consumed by the diverse ethno-cultural groups in Canada's major cities, which are reported to be the most multicultural in the world? Anecdotally, one might assume the generation gaps are greater, and media consumption habits, particularly among older generational groups, differ from mainstream North American consumption patterns. For example, hard-copy Chinese newspapers, as well as those in other languages, are flourishing while English-language dailies struggle. There's definitely room for more study here.

Media Relations in French Canada

Canada is, of course, a bilingual country, and media and public relations professionals must be aware of this fact. For English-speaking practitioners, the Quebec market poses many challenges, such as ensuring translations are properly done, as well as paying attention to many sociocultural differences. The following section, which was contributed by Daniel Granger, addresses the situation.

What is French Canada?

French Canada refers to a reality based on strong historical roots. "French Canadian" generally refers to the descendants of French colonists who arrived in New France in the 17th and 18th centuries. Today, there are French Canadians in various provinces, but Quebec has the largest such population.

The Official Languages Act came into force in 1969, and gave English and French equal status in all operations and services provided by the federal government. *Official bilingualism* is the term used to describe the policies, constitutional provisions, and laws that give English and French a special legal status in Canada's courts, Parliament and other federal institutions. The 1982 Constitution Act provides detailed guarantees for the equal status of the two official languages in the Canadian Charter of Rights and Freedoms.

French Canada Today

French is the mother tongue of more than seven million Canadians (22 per cent of the entire population), most of whom live in Quebec where they represent about 80 per cent of that province's population. The sole official language in Quebec is French following the adoption of the French Language Charter by the National Assembly in August 1977.

About one million Francophones live in other provinces. In New Brunswick, they represent one-third of the population of this officially bilingual province. Manitoba and Ontario have significant French-speaking communities while one will find much smaller communities in Alberta, Nova Scotia and Saskatchewan. The number and variety of institutions that support these communities are closely linked to their respective sizes.

As is the case with many other languages, French is spoken in a variety of regional dialects, the most important being Quebec French and Acadian French (prevalent in the Maritime provinces).

What about Quebec?

Quebec is the largest Canadian province in area, and the second largest in population with about 8.4 million people. Quebec is a mainly French-speaking society, and the defence of its language and culture colours all politics in the province.

Quebec's economic vitality is based on a number of factors, including abundant natural resources, low-cost hydroelectric power, a highly educated and skilled workforce, and innovative and dynamic IT, multimedia, life science and aerospace industries.

The people of Quebec live mostly in the south of the province, in cities located along the St. Lawrence River. Montreal, Canada's second largest city, and Quebec City, the province's capital, are the two largest metropolitan areas.

Quebec is listed among the most attractive tourist destinations in the world. Approximately ten million tourists visit the province each year.

Quebec has been very prominent on the Canadian sports scene with the Montreal Canadiens' 24 Stanley Cup wins, the Montreal Alouettes' seven CFL Grey Cup championships, the Laval University Rouge-et-Or football club's 10 Vanier Cups, and several Olympic champions, including Alexandre Despatie (diving), Clara Hughes (speed skating, cycling), Alexandre Bilodeau (acrobatic skiing), Jasey-Jay Anderson (show surfing), Charles Hamelin (speed skating), and Jennifer Heil (acrobatic skiing).

Quebec has also developed its own distinct cultural and artistic character thanks to its location at the crossroads between Europe and North America, the influence of several aboriginal traditions and its cultural diversity. As the only majority French-speaking society in North America, Quebec is fiercely attached to its language and culture.

Quebec has produced numerous artists who have achieved international recognition, including Félix Leclerc, Le Cirque du Soleil, Céline Dion, Robert Lepage, Luc Plamondon, Richard Desjardins, Karkwa, Leonard Cohen, Patrick Watson, Rufus Wainwright, Simple Plan, Oscar Peterson, Oliver Jones, and Arcade Fire.

In targeting Quebecers, one must ensure that the Quebec spokesperson is someone who resonates with the intended audience—a cultural figure for a cultural campaign, a sports personality for a campaign targeted at beer and soft drink drinkers, and so on.

Beyond the French Language

Failing to communicate with Quebecers in their own language is a fatal mistake.

Communicating with Quebec and other francophone parts of Canada does not mean simply translating an English news release, copy or voiceover into French. Because Quebec's differences are cultural and not merely linguistic, one must be acutely attuned to this culture to really understand this target audience and adapt strategies and messages accordingly.

A 1991 Ogilvy and Mather study found that Quebecers, particularly Montrealers, differ from Ontarians in that they tend to spend more on goods and services that provide instant gratification rather than on homes or other durables items.

Quebecers pay much more attention to food and anything that offers a healthy, wholesome lifestyle. They consume a lot more broadcast media than Ontarians and are far more loyal to their cultural roots in what they watch. All of the top ten TV shows in Quebec are produced there. Ontarians in contrast tend to favour US-produced shows. Quebecers participate in more winter sports and outdoor activities in general, and travel far less for pleasure outside of their province than their counterparts in Ontario.

This same note of caution should apply to other francophone communities in Canada even though they tend to live, develop and behave as minority groups in a predominantly English-speaking world. They expect that their differences will be respected, even though they are more accustomed to receiving materials that have been directly translated from English.

Another study comparing advertising in English Canada and Quebec found interesting differences in the messages and tactics used by companies. French-language ads tended to be more emotional than ones in English, which tended to be more informational.[10]

According to many surveys, Quebecers tend to favour the role of government in ensuring equal and readily accessible services (health,

10. Michel Laroche et al., "Cultural Differences in Environmental Knowledge, Attitudes, and Behaviours of Canadian Consumers," *Canadian Journal of Administrative Sciences* 19:3 (2002): 267–282.

education, social, justice, etc.) to all citizens. They tend to place less value on individuality and personal achievement than do their counterparts elsewhere in the country. That said, Quebecers do share many values with English-speaking Canadians, a point that should not be forgotten.

Whenever possible, one should hire on-the-ground public relations counsel, whether in Montreal, Quebec City or elsewhere in the province. Translating English campaign material into French should be done by someone with an intimate knowledge of the targeted audience's values and an awareness of possible regional differences. Usually it is preferable to create an original message than a literal translation, given differences in audience. Either way, you should allow for this step, ideally adding a week for it to be done properly.

In terms of media relations in a French-speaking market, messaging should be delivered whenever possible by a local bilingual spokesperson, and a local dateline should be included whenever possible. Media relations techniques tend to be more traditional with voice follow-up and face-to-face communications more prevalent.

If possible, messaging from outside sources should be tested, whether by in-province focus groups or other research methods.

Canada is one of the most multicultural countries on this planet, and its three biggest urban areas (Toronto, Montreal and Vancouver) are among the most multicultural in the world. Significant populations speak Chinese, Korean, and south Asian languages as their mother tongues, with vibrant corresponding news media; wherever possible in terms of budget and relevancy, media relations should be conducted in these languages as well.

Whether you are targeting Canadians who speak French, English, or other languages, specific research into your market is essential if your campaign is to succeed.

Preamble to Media Lists

Spend the research dollars and time to research your target audiences carefully. "Know your audience" is an age-old adage.

Mainstream news media such as daily newspapers and network television will often reach many of your target audiences. But don't overlook the many vertical, extremely targeted media outlets such as magazines (both print and digital), local or specialized TV shows, email newsletters, blogs and podcasts that can reach your target audience(s) more directly.

Ensure your media messages are in multimedia format suitable for television, radio, print and online media outlets so your message gets to your target audiences in a variety of ways.

Often, an integrated campaign that provides messaging towards the editorial (i.e., news) side can be augmented later with advertising. Display advertising in smaller circulation media outlets is not expensive. This is yet another way to hit that target audience with your messaging.

How to Build a Media List

The first part of building a media list is strategic—determine whom you are targeting with your message. Often your desired target audiences are diverse, so this should be clearly defined before beginning to build your media list.

The next step is getting in touch with a variety of suppliers out there who sell media lists and can customize them to your needs. Product offerings include one-time list purchases or subscriptions. These may be expensive, but invaluable to a successful media relations campaign.

It's always a good idea to purchase lists from a number of different sources, especially if you're starting out in a new media niche. To ensure your media list is as complete as possible, plan on calling and confirming information yourself at key media outlets.

My tactical philosophy is to get the news out in a variety of ways. I recommend combining direct email dissemination from your own ISP (with your name on the email) with the use of paid wire services and hard copy materials sent by mail or courier. This way you will ensure the targeted news media have seen your message. When purchasing media lists, make sure they contain phone numbers, email addresses (the best are those that go directly to journalists and not to general in-boxes) and mail addresses.

Finally, you should update the list constantly. Utilize email bounce backs as a warning you have wrong information or have been hit by a spam filter. As well, never underestimate the power of an old-fashioned phone call to the media outlet's reception desk.

Media Relations Planning: The Case Study

Plans are the core of the case study, which I highly recommend practitioners get in the habit of using as early in their careers as possible. In turn, the case study is the core of a proper wrap-up report. Highlights of such a report are key messaging and, of course, budget. Budget is paramount. Try very hard to get parameters out of internal or external clients.

Finally, gather or create as much research as possible about the relevant target audiences. It all starts there. Once target audiences are determined and fleshed out as much as possible, communications to those audiences through targeted media can be created.

Proposal Structure

A proposal for a media relations campaign (whether to an external or internal client) will generally include the following components:

- Preamble/introduction
- Objectives or goals (build in measurement paradigm here)
- Situational analysis or strategic considerations
- Key messaging
- Target audiences
- Target markets
- Target media
- Recommended strategies
- Recommended tactics
  - Web site recommendations
  - Media coaching
  - News release electronic distribution
  - Proactive/reactive media relations
  - Matte article distribution (ready-to-use articles)
  - Media monitoring/wrap-up report
- Timelines
- Budget cost estimate preamble (explain fees and disbursements)
- Budget cost estimate
- Biographies

The Intangible Benefits of Media Training

Besides preparing strategic key messaging and practising that messaging on camera, media training offers other, more intangible benefits.

First of all, the theory portion of a good media training course helps reduce news media illiteracy, which manifests itself either in clients being terrified of the news media or too arrogant with them, treating them as just another marketing communications function for hire. Teaching executives the difference between advertising and editorial, and the inherent danger of underestimating the power of the news media, tends to promote humility. Explaining that an advertising buy does not guarantee media coverage, even in the smallest trades, is surprisingly illuminating for some executives.

Conversely, once trainees understand the "information as commodity" concept, they tend to relax more when they fully understand their role in that two-way relationship. On-camera practising of key messaging and general Q&A's reduces fear, promotes humility, and increases media literacy. Allowing trainees to interview their colleagues, to play journalist, helps them to better understand the role the news media play and the challenges they face. It can also better identify potential information quagmires, since no one generally knows their business better than the trainees themselves, including all the areas that are problematic.

Media training can also greatly enhance the reputation of in-house media relations functions and officers by teaching potential spokespersons how difficult the art and science of media relations really is—that successful media relations is a complicated mix of newsworthy content, access, and timing and context. The training can become a useful opportunity to fully explain media relations protocol, and how breaching this protocol can become quite career limiting! It also introduces the in-house or external media relations team to the executive/spokesperson team, and provides a full day where they can work together and get to know each other and respect each other's roles and responsibilities, opportunities and challenges.

One of the greatest frustrations of media relations specialists, and the news media, is the slow response to interview or information requests. Yes, executives in private or public sector entities are as inundated as the media with information via email, voice mail, hard copy and social channels. But often executives don't understand the rapid timelines the news media operate under; they don't understand how quickly something ceases to be "news" or how quickly the media may lose interest in a proactive media relations venture or get frustrated during a reactive one.

The media training experience, when done in a proactive, co-operative style, can also serve as a team-building exercise. The on-camera experience can pull a group together since it can be as intimidating as climbing a wall or scaling a rope bridge, or other popular team-building exercises. Media training often brings together mid-to-senior level executives from different divisions who otherwise only see each other at sales conventions or work-related social gatherings.

Some executives I've media trained have told me how they have successfully applied some of the theory and practical media relations tips to other non-media audiences, such as problematic teenagers or unresponsive customer service departments. And we all know how tough some non-media audiences can be!

We are trained from an early age to always "answer the question" when asked by teachers, parents or other superiors. However, the organizational/news media interface is a two-way flow of information, and information is a commodity to news media. Below are some questions you have every right to ask the journalist before committing to an interview, if you do not have access to PR counsel. If you do, you can deflect those intrusive contacts; if a journalist does get around PR counsel (which some may try to do), then refer them back to proper contacts as per protocol.

Pre-Interview Questions

- In what section of the newspaper or on what TV or radio program, social media platform or website will the report appear?
- Will the interview be used for an immediate news story, or for a longer feature?
- What's the purpose of the interview and when will it be aired/printed?
- What is the angle of the interview and the report you're preparing?
- Will the interview be live or taped (for broadcast only)?
- How long will the interview last and where do you want to conduct it?
- Who precisely is the audience?
- Who else are you interviewing on the subject?
- What is your deadline?
- What is your telephone number and email address so I can get back to you?
- Media monitor that journalist and outlet to ascertain their usual background, attitude and treatment of interviewees.

Interview Tips

- Be media trained and have your key messages and response statements memorized.
- Never say anything "off-the-record" and be wary of providing "background" information. However, in certain cases, working with non-disclosure agreements ("NDA's") can be beneficial to both parties.
- Never say "no comment." Try saying something like: "When I have more information, I will be in a better position to respond."
- Review recent news coverage on the interview subject so you are as well informed as possible.
- Take your time before answering questions. Pauses can be to your advantage as a tool.
- Adhere to the under-10-second quote rule.
- Record your interview if possible.
- If you don't know the answer, admit it. Promise to get back to the journalist later with the answer if possible.
- If a question is negative, do not repeat the negative; always counter with a positive.
- Correct any erroneous or misleading information in a question without repeating the negative before you go on to answer the question.
- Keep your cool, no matter what.
- Listen carefully to the interviewer. If you did not understand or hear the question, or if you were asked multiple questions, ask them to repeat themselves.
- Maintain eye contact.
- Let the situation dictate your demeanour (and keep that demeanour throughout).
- Don't answer in monosyllables such as "yes" or "no."
- Don't speculate on hypothetical questions.
- Don't use trade-speak or marketing jargon or get too technical.
- Don't ever ask to review an article or broadcast story in advance of publication.

Types of Interviewers

The Machine Gunner: Asks several questions at once, quite quickly. The best way to deal with this kind of interviewer is to answer the question you want to with a key message.

The Interrupter: Asks another question, or interrupts before you're finished. If you have tightly prepared key messages (10 seconds or less) you should not have too much of a problem. You can also deal with this kind of interviewer by saying: "Please let me finish my answer" or "Just a moment, please," and complete your statement.

The Paraphraser: Dangerous, because they can cleverly but misleadingly paraphrase what you have said. Listen carefully to their paraphrases, and correct them immediately if they stray too far from your statements or contain misinformation.

The Dart Thrower: This type of interviewer will pin negative labels on you, such as: "Aren't you just trying to gain good publicity by donating all that computer equipment to that inner-city school?" Correct negatives with positives such as: "The school was very grateful for our equipment and now can have more online access because of it."

The Hostile Interviewer: Answer their key question only. Don't get mad! Perhaps ask them to repeat their question. Use pauses. Or re-phrase the question in your own words, then answer it. Be firm, but polite.

The Overly Friendly Interviewer: Sometimes they just like meeting people. Or they can be disarming you, particularly during the pre-interview, and then go "in for the kill" when recording. Be cautious, but not too cold. You do not want to offend them if they are being genuine.

The "Last Minute" Interviewer: Take control of the interview. Correct this poor soul only if absolutely necessary to avoid embarrassing him or her. Be prepared for ill-informed questions. This interviewer appears to know very little about the subject because he probably has not had time to prepare and was handed a last-minute assignment with no background. You can use his lack of knowledge to your advantage if managed carefully.

Types of Interviews and Tips

Telephone (and Recorded) Interviews: Can be the most dangerous because you can be the most relaxed in your own environment, or distracted, for example, when talking on a mobile phone while driving in heavy traffic. Avoid the temptation of doing the interview immediately. If possible, record the interview. Also ask the interviewer if you're being recorded.

The Rules on Recording: A journalist must inform you that you are being recorded for broadcast. In Canada, however, a reporter can record you without telling you if the interview is not to be broadcast, so everything is "on-the-record." In some US states, the law requires that both parties to a recording must agree to its release, even if the contents are just to be transcribed and not broadcast.

The Scrum: Is trade slang to describe when a number of journalists gather around you for comment. The scrum is very common after court appearances, or in politics, for example, in the parliamentary lobby after Question Period. The media may also scrum you at public appearances such as speeches, panel discussions, or regulatory meetings, particularly where microphone feeds are not supplied. Often scrums are held to get specific answers to specific questions, and to get better quality "sound bites" or quotes from you.

Reporters will compete with each other to get the microphone in your face. They sometimes take on the appearance of an angry mob. But never, ever, try to avoid a scrum. The video of you running away can be very damaging.

Reporters will often ask questions all at once. Choose the one you like. If you are in the middle of answering an undesirable question and another more positive question is asked, turn to that reporter and answer their question.

Take your time in answering and remember your key messages. If you don't understand a question, ask for it to be repeated. Because scrums are a form of pack journalism, pauses can be used to elicit other questions. Other reporters will always fill in pauses with questions. Don't forget the competitive nature of the journalists surrounding you and the fact that they work in different formats.

Interview Tips for Television

- Focus on the interviewer, not the camera.
- Ignore camera operators and other technicians as they go about their business.
- You should consider yourself "on-the-record" from the moment you enter the TV station until you're in your car leaving the studio. Asides can be heard and recorded in-studio, or even in the hallways or "green room."
- Never talk over the interviewer.
- Avoid "ums" and "ahs."
- Allow camera operators to get shots wherever they want, and don't necessarily expect the interview to take place in your office behind your desk.
- Dress for the occasion. If you're in the plant, wear a hard hat and coveralls. If you're at an outdoor event, wearing a business suit may not be appropriate.
- Don't be alarmed by "re-asks," when the camera-operator moves behind you and the reporter asks many of the same questions covered previously. This is for editing purposes or they may be looking for a tighter quote.

CHEK NEWS BC FERRIES INTERVIEW/CAM ABBOTT (FLICKR)

- Stick to your original answers and stay serious. No bravado or silliness during these re-asks. You are still being recorded.
- Concentrate on the interviewer at all times. Look him or her in the eye. Use natural hand movements as emphasis to your answers. Listen carefully and actively. And never look into the camera (unless you are doing a remote TV panel discussion).
- Avoid clasping hands tightly, gripping the sides of chairs or tables, playing with pencils, water glasses, buttons, looking around, closing your eyes, blinking too much, swivelling in your chair—all these give the impression of nervousness, boredom and even lying.
- Sit straight and avoid moving. Leaning slightly forward in your chair gives the impression that you're alert and in control.
- Wait until the TV lights are off, the red lights on the cameras are off, and the technician removes your lapel microphone. Then you may relax slightly, but only slightly. Manage your demeanour carefully, because the cameras often stay on you and the host for several minutes while the show's credits roll. Nothing is worse than the audience seeing you and the host smiling after a serious interview. Never say "I'm glad that's over," or "How did I do?"

How to Dress for TV

- Wear medium tones—no pure white shirts. White can wash you out and make you look pale. Avoid red or black shirts, too.
- Royal blue is a great suit colour with light blue as a good shirt colour.
- Men should wear executive-length (high) socks.

- Avoid patterns that have stripes, plaids and checks. Such patterns are not "camera-friendly."
- Avoid highly polished jewellery for the same reason.
- Shoes should be dark and well shined.
- Avoid new haircuts, but ensure hair is neatly groomed.
- Skirts should be long enough to cover the knees when seated. Avoid wrap-around skirts. Embarrassing gaps may appear on-camera. Pant suits are preferred by many spokeswomen.
- Watch for bulges in jackets caused by electronic devices, pocketbooks, keys etc.
- Normal make-up should be worn. In-studio interviews are usually attended by professional make-up artists.
- If you're on a media tour, have a wardrobe organized in advance to avoid bothersome decisions when on the road.
- Before going on air, eat lightly and avoid coffee, tea and alcohol (they dry up your mouth).

Interview Tips for Radio

- Radio can be a deceptive medium. You may think your voice has energy and vitality, but by the time it makes its way through all the technology to a listener's speaker, your voice sounds flat.
- Remember to put about twice as much action into your voice as you would in normal conversation, and it will sound full of energy (but natural) on the receiving end.
- Vary your pitch, tone, rate and volume.
- Overall, sound conversational and personal. Radio is a very personal medium.
- If doing a radio interview over the telephone, keep your mouth about six inches away to avoid the popping sounds caused by letters like "p," because most telephone microphones are of poorer quality.
- Don't be disappointed if the interview took hours, but the resulting story is only about 45 seconds in length. Brevity rules radio news these days. Remember, your quotes, or sound bites (clips), should be short—less than ten seconds.

Interview Tips for Print

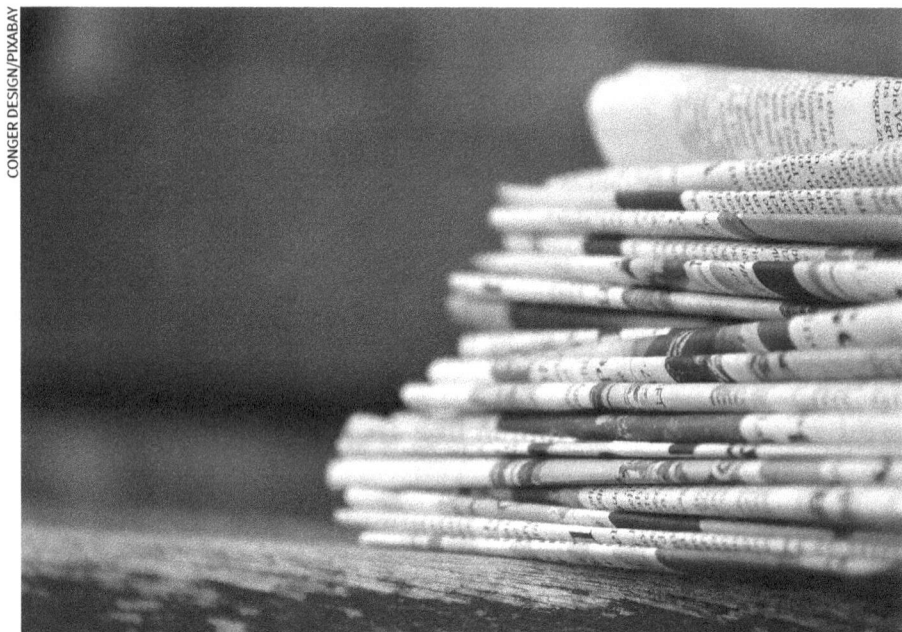

- These interviews are generally longer than radio or television interviews, but remember, a TV interview can last half a day and yield only a few seconds of airtime …
- Print reporters generally require far more detail than radio or TV.
- It is common for a reporter to use a recorder. They should not mind if you do as well. Remember to keep the machines as far apart as possible to avoid feedback.
- Don't complain if some of the quotes aren't exact or some of the facts are slightly misinterpreted. Complaining will only antagonize the reporter. If there is a serious error or misquote, please see my advice in a later section on corrections.
- Be prepared for the reporter (or a researcher) to call back to check quotes and facts. If the reporter indicates the article will be published the next day, be reachable until after that newspaper's bedtime (anywhere from 6 p.m. to 10 p.m.). However, do not hand out your personal telephone (or mobile) number. Use a third party, such as public relations counsel, to coordinate such requests after hours.

Key Messages

- Key messages are 10- to 15-second sound bites that are memorable, to the point, and, where possible, colourful. Since most people only retain 10 per cent of the information they receive, messages must be concise and memorable.
- Key messages contain the main message you want to communicate.
- Key messages must be newsworthy. For example: "This is the first helicopter of its kind to not have a tail rotor, therefore it's among the quietest and safest on the market."
- Key messages should contain a call to action when warranted. For example: "Education spending on learning resources is now less than a half-cent of every education dollar. We want that figure tripled!"
- Localize your key message when necessary. For example: "Calgarians can practice proper hand washing by ensuring the antibacterial soap is lathered for 30 seconds."
- Paint a picture with your words.
- Use everyday language and avoid technical talk or other jargon and acronyms.
- Back up your key messages with facts, such as case studies, surveys, statistics or third party experts or authorities. Making an analogy is another back-up method and using personal experience humanizes your message.
- You should have no more than three key messages for an interview.
- Get into your key message as soon as possible and use it at every opportunity. However, try to do so while answering the question at the same time!
- Key messages should be positive.
- When you have prepared your key messages, print them out in over-sized print (14 to 16 point) on cue cards and have them by your side in preparation for and during telephone interviews. If you are going to have a face-to-face interview, have your key messages memorized.

Sample Media Training Agendas

AGENDA
FULL-DAY MEDIA TRAINING

10:00–10:05 a.m.: Welcome and introduction

10:05–11:35 a.m.: Theory
- Definition of public relations
- Definition of news media; brief discussion of each medium
- Current state of the news media
- What journalists want
- News hole concept: news as commodity
- News hole statistics
- News fence and the relationship between editorial and advertising
- News spotlight concept: news trendiness and pack journalism
- Newsworthiness concept
- Proactive and reactive media relations and differences
- Key messaging
- How to generate news
- Media relations protocols (customized to the organization)

11:35–12:00 p.m.: Lunch break

Afternoon: Spokespersons On-Camera
12:00–12:45 p.m.: Video review
12:45–12:50 p.m.: Interview #1
12:50–12:55 p.m.: Interview #2
12:55–1:00 p.m.: Interview #3
1:00–1:05 p.m.: Interview #4

1:05–1:25 p.m.: Interview reviews

1:25–1:35 p.m.: Interview #1
1:35–1:45 p.m.: Interview #2
1:45–1:55 p.m.: Interview #3
1:55–2:05 p.m.: Interview #4

2:05–2:25 p.m.: Break

2:25–3:25 p.m.: Final interviews; review
3:25–4:00 p.m.: Key message review; questions

Sample Media Training Agendas

<u>AGENDA</u>
<u>HALF-DAY MEDIA TRAINING</u>

1:00–1:05 p.m.: Welcome and introduction

1:05–2:00 p.m.: Theory
- Definition of public relations
- Definition of news media; brief discussion of each medium
- Current state of the news media
- What journalists want
- News hole concept: news as commodity
- News hole statistics
- News fence and the relationship between editorial and advertising
- News spotlight concept: news trendiness and pack journalism
- Newsworthiness concept
- Proactive and reactive media relations and differences
- Key messaging
- How to generate news
- Media relations protocols (customized to the organization)

2:00–2:15 p.m.: Break

Spokespersons On-Camera
2:00–2:45 p.m.: Video review
2:45–2:50 p.m.: Interview #1
2:50–2:55 p.m.: Interview #2
2:55–3:00 p.m.: Interview #3

3:00–3:15 p.m.: Interview reviews

3:15–3:25 p.m.: Interview #1
3:25–3:35 p.m.: Interview #2
3:35–3:45 p.m.: Interview #3

3:45–4:30 p.m.: Round #3 interviews; review
4:30–5:00 p.m.: Key message review; questions

What the News Media Want in Canada

- For news releases to be concise—300 to 400 words in length or shorter.
- For news to be on an electronic platter—in electronic format for easy editing and re-packaging.
- For images and video to be easily accessible but high quality.
- For spokespeople to come to them—electronically and in person. News conferences are generally too time-consuming. And to be able to quote the spokesperson!!!!
- For news to be of interest to a given media outlet's audience.
- For there to be a correlation between the electronic media kit, news releases, web site, photography and videography.
- For the web site to have an easily accessible, non-passworded media section as well as high-resolution photography (300 dpi, 8X10 JPEGs) and video (MPEG).
- For news releases to be newsworthy.
- For news releases and media advisories to be distributed regularly.
- For all English news copy to be translated into French.
- For information to be distributed both directly to media via email as well as through a paid wire service, where budget permits, so media are hit with the messaging at least twice to overcome danger of messaging lost in the inundation media face today. Ideally, hard copy delivery by mail or courier as well.
- For designated spokespersons and PR practitioners to be always ready to deal with last-minute media requests. If we can't service media in a timely manner, our competition will!

The Medium Is the Message

The truth of Canadian communication scholar Marshall McLuhan's old adage that "the medium is the message"—the title of this chapter—is evident in the recent transformation of news releases. The modern news release (no longer a "press release" unless you intend to send it only to print media) continues to evolve in tandem with new developments in information technology. In particular, the advent of the social media news release (with links, embedded video and audio, etc.) and smartphone and tablet technology has had a great impact on the news release as a form of communication.

News media surveyed by this author consistently want news releases that are short (300 words or less) and interactive, with direct URLs to enable the easy, non-password-protected access to high-resolution images, audio clips and video. The rapid progress of digital broadcast media has created inexpensive opportunities to capture and park broadcast quality audio clips, video clips at these designated URLs as well. Cumbersome backgrounders, PDFs and other support information such as biographies and white papers can also be parked at these URLs.

Organizational web sites should have "newsrooms" (the ideal location is the top left of the page to match journalistic graphic interface design) that not only contain news releases but also high-resolution images, broadcast quality audio and video clips, and background documents. Ideally, text should also be available in both Word and PDF formats, so media are served as quickly as possible in the format they prefer. Many "branch-plant" organizations often adopt third-party URLs to avoid delays and other issues with home-office webmasters.

With smartphone technology being widely adopted by the news media, there is only so much scroll-down capability so the news release should definitely fit in that window and run between 200 and 300 words, or less.

The creation of hybrid (print and broadcast) newsrooms due to media mergers and the electronic inundation of news locally, nationally and globally, make brevity of news releases more important than ever before. For years, I've tried to refine a style that is between print and broadcast so it is amenable to both media.

News release content is also paramount. There is little time for clichés these days. Words such as "state-of-the-art" and "world-class" tend to get a release deleted quickly. There is no room for hyperbole and puffery, and false claims may be closely scrutinized by the federal government. Highlighting and bolding is "so last century," and quotes should be included only if they continue the story. Although providing quoted names often helps in the media monitoring search-engine process, it is imperative that the person quoted or a designated back-up be readily available for rapid response interviews.

Of course, a news release is for immediate distribution, so why apply the pre-Internet concept of "for immediate release"?

The prominence of search engines in getting the story to all corners of the Internet has made it also necessary to spend extra time matching keywords in the release (the higher up in the copy the better) to Internet meta-tags, so when the paid wire gets the news release into cyberspace, the search engines will snag it.

As well, pay special attention to the subject line in the email. It must fit the window and capture the essence of the story. Other email tips: cut and paste your text into the email and never send attachments unless asked to do so; many newsroom spam filters will kill it instantly if you do. Always BCC (blind carbon copy) the media in your email, so they don't get a whole page of email addresses. This drives some of them to distraction. As well, be aware that many spam filters will reject emails that are BCC'ed to more than 25 addresses.

When following up with news media, email is often the preferred method these days. A few rounds should get you a high response rate. The telephone is considered more and more an evil interruption by many journalists and should be reserved for emergencies or the rare personal touch when welcomed. Never call after 4 p.m. unless you are returning a journalistic query.

A former editor-in-chief of The Canadian Press, Scott White, considers highly aggressive PR people who call multiple editors with the same pitch "time bandits." Enough said. One final tip for your news release writing: adhere to the *Canadian Press Style Guide* and its companion book *Caps and Spelling*.

Make that News Release Newsworthy!

When writing a news release, it's very important to follow the *five W's of news*: who, what, why, where, when. One can also add Rudyard Kipling's "how" ("The Elephant's Child"). Always ask yourself the questions: "Does it need a news release? Does it warrant a media advisory? Is this news?"

Keep the news release to about 300 to 400 words, one to 1½ printed pages maximum. The trend today is towards shorter. I envision the 50-word news release in the near future, with longer copy, such as waivers, placed at specific URLs, as well as backgrounders, boilerplates, photos, video, and survey results.

Write a News Release, Not an Advertisement

These are the key elements of a news release:

- Subject line: An art form in itself in the email world!
- Headline
- Subhead (if warranted)
- Dateline
- Lead: The "5 W's" but not necessarily all five
- Backups to lead, i.e., the rest of the W's
- Quotes: Prefer two sentences
- Closer: Final fact, strong ending
- Boilerplate (the "about the organization" section)
- URLs for backgrounders, fact sheets, and longer stuff
- URLs for images, downloadable broadcast video
- Contacts: be reachable, have a back-up

News Release Distribution Methods

News releases can be distributed in a variety of ways:

- Direct via email
- Direct via mail (this traditional channel offers new efficacy)
- Direct via fax (when requested, but waning)
- Paid wire services (for example, Cision)

Following is a sample news release announcing the publication of this book.

NEWS RELEASE

Media relations textbook provides 'toolbox' for public relations specialty

Toronto, ON, June 1, 2019 – Centennial College Press is pleased to release the third edition of Mark Hunter LaVigne's book on media relations, *Proactive Media Relations: A Canadian Perspective.*

The third edition is a significant update to the first and second editions, published in 2007 and 2011 respectively. LaVigne, an accredited public relations professional (APR) and member of the Canadian Public Relations Society's College of Fellows since 2010, has been a media relations specialist throughout his 28-year career in public relations. Like many in this specialty, he is a former journalist, spending five years in radio news in Calgary, Edmonton and Toronto after graduating with a Master of Arts in Journalism from Western University.

The book is based on years of experience in the college classroom as well. LaVigne has taught media relations and other public relations disciplines in colleges and universities including Seneca at York, Ryerson University, Western University, Centennial College and Humber College as well as delivering guest lectures and workshops widely across Canada.

"*Proactive Media Relations* covers the basics of media relations practice, and nicely balances traditional media relations (the news conference and news release for television, newspapers and radio) and working with digital and social media to get the message out in more channels," says William Wray Carney in his foreword to the book. "Regardless of whether you're working with traditional or newer media, the main elements of media relations remain the same: Define your market as narrowly as possible, determine the means of communications by which they receive information, craft messages that resonate with your target audience, send them out through the appropriate media channels, and engage your audience."

Carney is the long-time author of *In the News*, a groundbreaking work in media relations recently published by University of Alberta Press in its third edition. LaVigne is now a co-author of *In the News* and, in fact, wrote *Proactive Media Relations* as a companion to that book.

LaVigne also wrote the chapter on media relations in Carney's book, *Fundamentals of Public Relations and Marketing Communications* (University of Alberta Press, 2015).

"I have known Mark LaVigne for more than 20 years and have had the opportunity to collaborate with him on dozens of mandates with a variety of clients—businesses but also NPOs," says Daniel Granger, a recent appointee to the Order of Canada, in his introduction to *Proactive Media Relations*. "Mark is a great PR professional with strong personal values whose work ethic is exemplary. But it is in his particular field of expertise, media relations, that he excels."

Proactive Media Relations: A Canadian Perspective, third edition, is available now at a suggested list price of $30 through major book retailers and wholesalers. For more information, visit the Centennial College Press website at https://centennialcollegepress.com/.

About Centennial College Press

Centennial College Press publishes textbooks and learning resources as well as selected trade and professional titles. The Press is located in Toronto at the Story Arts Centre, a campus of Centennial College.

For more information, please contact:

David Stover
Publisher/Manager
Centennial College Press
416-289-5000, ext. 8605
https://centennialcollegepress.com

Case Studies

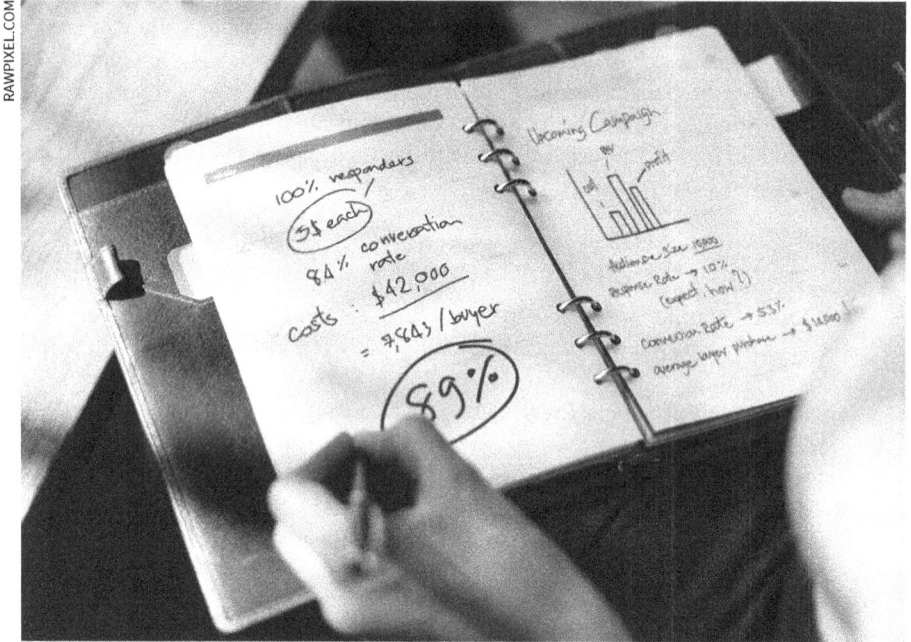

In the next section, I present sample case studies and related news releases that expand on the concepts discussed so far. A mix of for-profit and not-for-profit campaigns are included.

CrosSled Case Study

(Winner, CPRS Toronto ACE Awards: Bronze, Special Events, 2002)

Preamble

CrosSled's annual sales growth rate of 50 per cent per year over four seasons is based largely on awareness generated by media relations and print advertising. The total communications budget is approximately $30,000, which includes targeted media buys. In 2000/2001 season planning, PR counsel recommended that a grassroots style public event was needed to publicize the CrosSled product and sport (kicksledding). The Kortright Centre had come to CrosSled in its second season wanting to use our product as part of their public participation program. About six CrosSleds ended up being used quite successfully during the 1999/2000 season. CrosSled approached the Kortright in our third season in order to partner with them to hold the CrosSled Rendezvous.

Objectives

- To build brand equity among current customers and potential ones.
- To generate awareness through media coverage.

Strategy

Provide a fun-filled environment to stimulate grassroots enthusiasm and word-of-mouth endorsement for the product among current and potential customers.

Strategic Considerations

- Venue must offer outdoor winter amenities as well as indoor facilities.
- Venue must be known to media and easily accessible to media.
- Venue must be central point for all GTA customers.

Selected Venue and Timeframe (conducive timing for partner)

Kortright Centre, Sunday, January 14, 2001, 11 a.m. to 2 p.m.

Target Audiences

- Current CrosSled customers (via direct invite)
- Kortright newsletter recipients (via Kortright newsletter distribution)
- General winter enthusiasts (Kortright visitors)

Measurement

Number of attendees at event and quality and quantity of media coverage generated.

Challenges/Limitations

- Getting folks out in winter weather is challenging—either too cold or too warm (rain).
- Low budget
- Relatively new product and sport

Budget

- Fees: $3,375
- Disbursements: $5,775
- Total: $9,150

Event Elements

- Hard-packed trail for relay race, more serious race, and kids' scavenger hunt (for marshmallows)
- About a dozen sleds available for free demo, including handful of the new Racers
- BBQ for cookout (hot dogs, hamburgers, soft drinks, beer)
- Music available (Abba) via portable CD player
- Hired videographer to shoot video
- Prizes for event winners (CrosSled hats and scarves)
- CrosSled maintenance clinic
- Invited CrosSled partners (i.e., Wil Wegman, Canadian Ice Fishing Team)

Tactics

- Media advisory distributed via CNW one week prior (January 5) with repeats on the Friday and Saturday mornings. Media advisory also distributed directly via email to comprehensive media list.
- Videographer shot Beta quality video. Dubbed to Beta in field. Delivered by driver to all GTA TV outlets.
- Photographer shot on professional digital camera. Emailed to paid wire service from field.

Attending Media

City-tv, *Toronto Star*, *The Liberal* [Richmond Hill, Ont.], TVOntario

MEDIA ADVISORY

CrosSled Rendezvous at Kortright Centre to celebrate new sport in Canada

Unionville, ON, Monday, January 8, 2001 – The first annual CrosSled Rendezvous will be held at the Kortright Centre for Conservation in Woodbridge January 14, 2001 to gather together CrosSled enthusiasts and introduce the sport to the general public.

The CrosSled Rendezvous includes a scavenger hunt for kids, a relay race for adults, and a complimentary B-B-Q, all on CrosSleds of course! A number of CrosSleds will be available for demo purposes.

The CrosSled looks like a dogsled, with a seat affixed to the front of two ski rails with a handlebar attached to the top of the seat. The CrosSledder stands behind the seat, holding onto the handlebar. One foot is placed on a ski rail, while the other propels the sled forward with a kicking motion – hence the generic term kicksled or kicksledding.

CrosSled is a "150-year-old new invention" according to Knut Brundtland, a Norwegian Canadian who is dedicated to introducing the sport to North Americans. CrosSledding utilizes all of the muscle groups with excellent cardiovascular benefits and is second only to cross-country skiing for overall body development. Brundtland maintains the sport's low impact nature makes it an excellent cross-training activity, especially for those winter athletes with temporary injuries.

Canadians have adapted this Scandinavian device to a number of uses, according to Brundtland, including as a snowstroller for those with young children, a snow walker for seniors who want winter exercise but are afraid of dangerous ice conditions, a tackle box on skis for ice anglers to haul their equipment across the ice, and an inexpensive dog sled for dog owners who want to keep their canines, and themselves, active during winter months.

What: CrosSled Rendezvous
When: Sunday, January 14, 11 a.m. to 3:30 p.m.
Where: Kortright Centre for Conservation, 9550 Pine Valley Drive, Woodbridge (400 to Major Mackenzie Drive West, to Pine Valley Drive South)

For more information, please contact: *[Name, office phone, cell phone, and email addresses of PR, client, and third party if applicable]*

NEWS RELEASE

CrosSled Rendezvous at Kortright Centre celebrates new sport in Canada

Unionville, ON, Sunday, January 14, 2001 – Dozens of CrosSled enthusiasts gathered at the Kortright Centre for Conservation in Woodbridge today to celebrate their 150-year-old new sport.

The first annual CrosSled Rendezvous included a scavenger hunt for kids and a relay race for adults at the Kortright Centre's CrosSled Loop—trails cut through a field ideally suited for CrosSledding. Other events included a presentation by Canadian ice fishing guru Wil Wegman, who demonstrated how CrosSled helps his sport. Enthusiasts gathered around a bonfire, on their CrosSleds, to enjoy après CrosSled refreshments and bonhomie.

The CrosSled looks like a dogsled, with a seat affixed to the front of two ski rails with a handlebar attached to the top of the seat. The CrosSledder stands behind the seat, holding onto the handlebar. One foot is placed on a ski rail, while the other propels the sled forward with a kicking motion—hence the generic term kicksled or kicksledding.

Kicksledding has been a fixture in Norway, Finland and Sweden for a century and a half and Norwegian Canadian Knut Brundtland has dedicated himself to introducing the sport to North Americans. Brundtland says CrosSledding utilizes all of the muscle groups with excellent cardiovascular benefits and is second to cross-country skiing for overall body development.

Canadians have adapted this Scandinavian device for easy winter fun activities and for low impact fitness training. Other uses, according to Brundtland, include CrosSled as a snowstroller for those with young children, a snow walker for seniors who want winter exercise but are afraid of dangerous ice conditions, a tackle box on skis for ice anglers to haul their equipment across the ice, and an inexpensive dog sled for dog owners who want to keep their canines, and themselves, active during winter months.

For more details, visit CrosSled's web site at www.crossled.com. High-resolution images of the CrosSled product line-up and of CrosSleds being used by a variety of Canadians can be found and downloaded at www.crossled.com/press.

For more information, please contact: *[Name, office phone, cell phone, and email addresses of PR, client, and third party if applicable]*

Sunrise Soya Foods/Pete's Tofu
Launch Case Study
(Winner, CPRS Toronto ACE Awards: Bronze, New Product Launch, 2003)

Preamble

In December 2001, a campaign was developed by Hunter LaVigne Communications Inc. to promote the Pete's Tofu product launch, Vancouver-based Sunrise Soya Foods' expansion to eastern Canada and its Toronto plant opening.

Pete's Tofu was launched on Monday, May 13, 2002 with English, French and Chinese news releases with detailed media follow up. News releases were distributed to 280 targeted contacts and disseminated nationally (in English and French) by CNW Group. Media contacts were offered a comprehensive media kit (hard copy and electronic formats), product samples, product demonstrations, plant tours and video. The Toronto plant was officially opened September 24, 2002 with an event that attracted 20 media contacts, as well as 100 employees, their families, suppliers and regulators.

Objectives

- Raise awareness of new Pete's Tofu product line through media coverage.
- Raise awareness of Sunrise and its brand through plant opening event.
- Increase Sunrise brand awareness in Ontario and Quebec.

Strategy

Use a two-tiered approach—a product launch and then plant opening event four months later to create news media momentum, regionally and nationally, culminating in spot news after plant-opening event.

Strategic Considerations

- Although health benefits of soya are becoming better known amongst Canadian mass consumers, the benefits of tofu products are not as well known.
- Prior to the Pete's Tofu launch, awareness of Sunrise Soya products was high in western Canada, but negligible in Ontario and Quebec.
- The Toronto news marketplace is particularly inundated with information, as one of North America's largest urban areas that has been

considerably downsized in the past year through mergers, acquisitions and technological factors.

Target Audiences
- General consumers, including women aged 18–55-plus
- Vegetarians—general skew
- Bodybuilders/health trade
- Grocery store owners, managers, buyers

Target Media
- Business, food and family editors at major daily newspapers in Toronto, Ottawa, Montreal and Quebec City
- Business and food specialists/shows at mainstream radio and television outlets in Toronto, Montreal and Quebec, including cable cooking shows
- Food consumer and trade magazines
- Women's magazines
- Relevant web sites
- Food and cooking freelancers
- Ethnic media in Toronto and Montreal

Tactics
- Production of print photography and video to facilitate media coverage
- Electronic news kit and hard-copy media kit development and distribution, including extensive one-page backgrounders, recipes, cooking tips, photos, plant tour video clip and glossary of terms
- Dissemination of news release and backgrounders electronically via email and paid wire service (in English, French and Chinese)
- Plant media tours
- Live product drops and demonstrations to news and food media
- Follow up email and telephone calls
- Plant opening with Ontario Minister of Agriculture and Food, Chinese lion dance performance, cooking demonstrations by noted chefs and food samples as hooks

Measurement
Quantity and quality of media coverage, number of media attendees at event, product awareness studies and product sales.

Budget

Total budget was $61,166, with $47,566 for fees and $13,600 for disbursements.

Results

- Total of 21,396,964 first impressions generated (2,150.06 square inches generated with total of 58:45 broadcast minutes aired). Highlights included: two *Globe and Mail* photo features; local and national coverage on CBC, Global and CFTO (CTV), colour photo features in *Canadian Living* and *Homemakers*, and pick-up by The Canadian Press.
- Pete's Tofu consumer brand awareness among non-traditional tofu users in Ontario and Quebec went from zero to five per cent between May and August 2002, achieving a seven per cent market share in dollars in Canada (A.C. Nielsen). Sales are expected to exceed one million dollars in 2003.
- More than 100 guests, plus 20 news media, attended plant-opening event.

NEWS RELEASE

Sunrise opens new plant and launches new brand to meet growing demand for tofu

Toronto, ON, May 13, 2002 – To meet the growing interest in soyfoods, as well as a demand for convenient, ready-to-eat products, Sunrise Soya Foods is opening a new tofu manufacturing plant in Toronto to help facilitate the launch of their newest brand, "Pete's Tofu."

The Toronto plant, utilizing the latest in automated tofu manufacturing technology and quality control, is expected to employ more than 50 people by the time it's fully operational this fall. This second factory was needed to ease the production workload from their first plant (already run at full capacity in Vancouver) where 175 people are employed.

Helping "take the guesswork out of tofu" for mainstream consumers, Pete's Tofu features five innovative, ready-to-eat tofu products. Pete's "Tofu2Go" flavour-packed triangles with dipping sauce packs and "Peach Mango" and "Very Berry" naturally flavoured twin pack tofu desserts are intended to be a hit with consumers who don't know what to do with tofu.

"The demand for tofu among Canadians in Ontario and Quebec, and Americans in the eastern seaboard cities, is growing by about 15 per cent each year," says Peter Joe, General Manager and Chief Executive Officer of Sunrise Soya Foods, a 46-year-old tofu manufacturer headquartered in Vancouver. "Our new Toronto plant will reduce our shipping costs from B.C. to the East Coast, and extend our product shelf life since much of the tofu will now be made locally."

Sunrise is based in Western Canada, a home market in which it enjoys about 80 per cent market share and has been promoting tofu's health benefits and versatility in cooking for decades. As a culinary chameleon, tofu takes on the flavour of whatever ingredients with which it is used. Cumulative studies suggest that tofu consumption may lower LDL "bad" cholesterol levels, and, in turn, reduce the risk of heart disease. Research also indicates that tofu may prevent hormone-dependent cancers, ease menopausal symptoms and reduce the risk of osteoporosis. As a cholesterol-free source of protein, tofu also acts as a dairy, meat or egg substitute or complement in everyday recipes.

Sunrise Soya Foods was founded in 1956, and is Canada's largest tofu manufacturer and the fifth largest in North America. Currently, Sunrise employs more than 200 Canadians. Sunrise's brands and product offerings address health, mainstream and ethnic markets. Newcomer "Pete's Tofu," made with organic soybeans, is contained in consumer-friendly packaging, which features on-pack recipes. Sunrise has partnered with many grocery, health food and Asian stores in Canada and is expected to double or triple with expansion into the US markets.

To meet the growing interest in tofu, Sunrise offers two web sites in three languages and a toll-free Consumer Bean-Line at 1-800-661-2326. All Sunrise products are certified Kosher. For more information, go to www. sunrise-soya.com or www.petestofu.com.

- 30 -

For more information, please contact: *[Name, office phone, cell phone, and email addresses of PR, client, and third party if applicable]*

MEDIA ADVISORY

Sunrise Soya Foods to officially open new Toronto plant

Toronto, ON, September 13, 2002 – Sunrise Soya Foods, Canada's largest tofu manufacturer, will host a grand opening of its new Toronto manufacturing facility from 11 a.m. to 2 p.m., on Tuesday September 24th, offering savory luncheon fare by local chefs Nettie Cronish and Mark Jachecki.

The state-of-the-art, 30,000 square foot facility will be officially opened at 11:30 a.m. with a ceremonial Chinese lion dance, followed by a ribbon cutting by Peter Joe, General Manager and CEO of the 46-year-old family-owned firm. Helen Johns, Minister of Agriculture and Food, will also be in attendance.

During the culinary event, some 200 guests will be invited to tour the plant, learn about the tofu making process and view a history wall display about this "culinary chameleon's" escalating popularity as a fast, delicious and healthy addition to Canadian menus.

Sunrise Soya Foods employs more than 200 Canadians and is the fifth largest tofu manufacturer in North America. Its brands and product offerings address health, mainstream and ethnic markets. Newcomer "Pete's Tofu," made with organic soybeans, uses consumer-friendly packaging that features on-pack recipes to further expand awareness. Sunrise has partnered with many grocery, health food and Asian stores in Canada and the U.S. All Sunrise products are certified Kosher.

For more information, visit www.sunrise-soya.com or www.petestofu.com, or call the toll-free Consumer Bean-Line at 1-800-661-2326.

What: Grand opening of Sunrise Soya Foods new Toronto plant
When: Tuesday, September 24, 2002, 11 a.m.–2 p.m.
       Arrivals, refreshments and hors d'oeuvres: 11–11:30 a.m.
       Lion dance: 11:30–11:50 a.m.
       Ribbon cutting and opening remarks: 11:50 a.m.–12:05 p.m.
       Plant tours, culinary demonstrations and sampling: 12:05–2 p.m.
Where: 21 Medulla Ave., Toronto, ON, Tel.: 416-233-2337 (Medulla runs
       north off North Queen St. between Kipling and East Mall)
Who: Peter Joe, President and CEO, Sunrise Soya Foods
       Helen Johns, Minister of Agriculture and Food, Government of
       Ontario
       Peter Milczy, Ward 5 Councillor
       Nettie Cronish, vegetarian chef and cookbook author
       Mark Jachecki, executive chef, Presidential Gourmet Corporation

Schneiders Oh Naturel! Case Study

Preamble
Hunter LaVigne Communications (HLC) conducted a re-launch since the original product launched to media in spring 2004 without desired results.

Objective
To raise awareness of product line through media coverage.

Strategy
Through sampling and seasonal hook, re-introduce the product to larger news media audience.

Strategic Considerations
- Diverse target audiences requiring media relations specialists with language specific experience
- Now soft news because of spring program
- Large team to manage for both client and lead agency, HLC

Target Audiences
- Women 18–49 years old (emphasis on women 18–34 years)
- Young teenage girls
- Older baby boomers (male and female)
- Urban, professional, well-educated and affluent

Target Markets
- Toronto
- Montreal
- Calgary
- Vancouver

Target Media
- Major-market daily newspapers and wire service contacts (business, health and food)
- Consumer magazines (mainly women targeted, business, health and food editors and writers)
- Trades and business magazines (food, packaging, plant, grocery)

- Marketing publications/editors (both trades and dailies with some electronic and web)
- Ethnic media (print and broadcast)
- Freelancers (mainly food and health)

Tactics

- Sampling program to 250-plus news media (English, French, Chinese) with news release as well as direct email and paid wire dissemination (Marketwire (formerly CCNMatthews))
- Winter BBQ angle taken
- Integrated with launch of print and TV advertising along with feature article dissemination through News Canada

Measurement

Quantity and quality of media coverage

Budget

Total budget was $31,710, with $22,150 for fees and $9,560 for disbursements. Does not include sampling costs and shipping.

Results

- 12.2 million impressions including: *Soy Daily*, *Marketing* (magazine and online), *24 Heures* Montreal, *Calgary Sun*, CFTR 680 News (weekend run), *Le Soleil*, *Toronto Sun*, *Canadian Packaging*, *Food in Canada*, *Food Service & Hospitality*, *Grocer Today*, *Western Grocer*, *Toronto Star*, CBC Radio (national), *Vancouver Sun*, *The Record* (Kitchener-Waterloo), *Forever Young* magazine, *7 Jours*, *Capital Sante*, *L'actualite Alimentarie* and Chinese publications *Canadian Chinese Times*, *Ming Pao*, *Epoch Times*, *Calgary Trend Weekly*, *Calgary and Chinese Times*.
- The combination of advertising and public relations work propelled Oh Naturel into second place in unit and dollar share in the category eclipsing the more established BOCA brand. Share figures continued to show strength after both the PR and media campaigns were completed. Overall consumer sales doubled immediately following the campaigns to achieve over half a million consumer units in the first six months of 2005.
- Media Relations Ratings Point (MRRP) Score: 85 per cent

NEWS RELEASE

When you BBQ this winter, go Oh Naturel!

Kitchener, ON, January 13, 2005 – Canadians certainly love their BBQs, and show their dedication from coast-to-coast by lighting up the grill year-round. In fact, surveys show that almost one-fifth have fired up the BBQ at temperatures below minus 20 degrees Celsius. This year, Schneiders encourages Canadians to brave the cold "Oh Naturel!"

This passion for barbequing can now be combined with another popular past time: New Year's resolutions to lead healthier lifestyles. It makes perfect sense to use the Schneiders Oh Naturel!™ line of meatless burgers, wieners, ground round, chick'n strips, beef strips, chick'n nuggets, meatballs and chick'n burgers to help achieve this goal.

"Research showed that 80 per cent of burgers and wieners are consumed from the BBQ and yet most meatless products have performed poorly on the BBQ," says Tracey Peake, Marketing Manager, Schneider Foods. "We designed our meatless burgers and wieners specifically with the BBQ in mind knowing that they have to be juicy, flavourful and taste great off the grill."

Schneiders Oh Naturel!™ products are a good source of protein, contain all the goodness of soy, are lower in fat, low in or free of trans and saturated fats, cholesterol free, lower in calories and sodium and are a good source of fibre. They are available at major grocery stores across Canada, including Sobey's, A&P, Dominion, Safeway, Overwaitea/Save-On, IGA and Wal-Mart in the frozen, produce or meat sections.

The Schneiders Oh Naturel!™ products are produced in a new 20,000 square foot facility in Burnaby, B.C., dedicated to meatless products, employing 30 full and part-time employees.

"Schneiders is the first major brand to combine great taste, convenience and good nutrition in a 'centre of the plate' meat alternative," adds Peake. "These products are made with Schneiders care and attention to quality, so the products include an improved texture and great taste not normally associated with soy products."

For more than a century, the name "Schneiders" has been synonymous with great taste, tradition, and quality. Founded in 1890, the company now employs more than 5,500 people and has sales of more than $1 billion. Schneider Foods produces more than 1,000 products with operations across Canada. Schneider Foods was acquired by Maple Leaf in March 2004, and is an independent operating company of Maple Leaf Foods.

For more information, go to www.schneiderfoods.ca. A high-resolution product photo of Schneiders Oh Naturel!™ product packaging is parked at: *[add URL where material is located]*.

Winter BBQ Tips

Schneider Foods offers the following Winter BBQ tips to keep you safe this winter:

1.   Don't grill in your garage, even with the door open. Harmful fumes can accumulate.
2.   Wear an old parka or apron, including gloves, so you don't stink up or dirty your better outerwear and make sure you have a winter matt inside the entrance so you don't trudge snow and ice into living areas.
3.   Avoid wearing a scarf and a hat with dangling drawstrings while winter barbecuing, as they can catch on fire quite easily.
4.   Keep snow and ice off the barbecue and clear the snow around it regularly so it doesn't become slippery when the barbecue heats it up or freezes up afterwards.
5.   Invest in a good pliable plastic cover that will not break in very cold weather. Wait until the barbecue cools before placing the cover back on or it could melt onto the lid.
6.   Below minus 20 degrees Celsius (minus 4 degrees Fahrenheit), knobs and handles can become very brittle and break off, so handle with care and have small vice-grip pliers handy for knob and handle emergencies.
7.   Ensure your barbecue area is well lit so you can see what you're doing in the dark. Remember that many parts of Canada get dark in the winter BEFORE dinnertime. Headlamps work well if you don't have barbecue area lighting.
8.   Use a meat thermometer to check internal temperatures because cooking times will greatly vary between summer and winter.
9.   Have a spare propane tank filled in case the one that's connected to the barbecue runs out during cooking.
10. Never use a blowtorch to thaw out frozen tank fittings and never lick the barbecue lid to see if your tongue sticks.

For more information, please contact: *[Name, office phone, cell phone, and email addresses of PR, client, and third party if applicable]*

Yellow Brick House Pathway for Peace Case Study

Preamble

Yellow Brick House is a non-profit shelter for abused women and children and homeless women and children, serving York Region (north of Toronto). United Way funding had been cut drastically, so the shelter is dependent on the Ministry of Community and Social Services (COM-SOC) for most of its funding. It has to generate about $300,000 per year in self-raised funds to meet its current budget. Holding any kind of media or public event at the shelter was not possible due to security and privacy concerns. The Pathway for Peace, the brainchild of Mark LaVigne, APR, is a very simple concept. It is designed to refurbish a rundown public space. Through that space, a pathway of cobblestones is built and a monument erected. Then the cobblestones or "bricks" can be "sold" in kind. Once or twice a year a plaque is erected to honour those who bought bricks.

Objectives

- Generate awareness of Yellow Brick House and abuse/homeless issues through media coverage.
- Generate money through brick sales.

Strategy

Attract a noted celebrity to open the pathway so it can raise money and awareness at the same time.

Strategic Considerations

- Potential violence against the venue by enraged former partners was a concern. (The monument was firmly rooted ten feet deep and lighting was installed as a precaution.)
- Attracting enough initial donors of products and services to make the project financially viable (more than $100,000 worth of goods and services were donated).

Selected Celebrity

The then Lieutenant Governor of Ontario, the Honourable Hilary M. Weston, agreed to "launch" the pathway.

Target Audiences
York Region-based families and businesses.

Measurement
- Quality and quantity of media coverage generated over 1.5-year period
- Brick sales, since main marketing communications vehicle was media relations over the same period

Challenges/Limitations
- Lack of budget to purchase or generate marketing communications other than media relations and direct mailing to shelter donors
- Location of media events 60 kilometres north of downtown Toronto

Budget
- Fees: public relations counsel and project management was pro bono
- Disbursements: $32,860 including landscaping and pathway construction, three monument stones, engraving and placement, three sets of plaques

Event Elements/Critical Path
- Teaser photo-op event of monument arrival for engraving was held May 23, 2000.
- Launch event was held June 27, 2000 with the Honourable Hilary M. Weston and Aurora Mayor Tim Jones in attendance. Key invitees to launch included key COMSOC officials, other local politicos, more than 100 school children and dozens of Yellow Brick House staff, volunteer board members and former residents. Ribbon cutting/plaque unveiling conducted by Weston & Jones.
- Plaque commemoration events were held Sept. 26, 2000 and June 29, 2001 where plaques were unveiled on monument. Mayor Jones attended both.

Tactics
- Media advisory was distributed via paid wire and email one week prior to events.
- Videographer was hired at half rate for launch event where he shot Beta quality video, which was dubbed at downtown facility and delivered by driver to all GTA TV outlets.

- Photographer shot images on professional digital camera at all three events. Emailed to key local media each time.

Results

- More than six million first impressions have been generated in news media over 1.5-year period including local TV such as CKVR-TV, Shaw and Rogers, local newspapers such as the *Era Banner*, *Town Crier*, *Liberal* and *Auroran*, Global TV, and CBC Radio (five-minute documentary).
- The path paid for itself in six months. It so far has raised about $4,000 in profits that go directly into shelter revenues.

MEDIA ADVISORY

Pathway for Peace in Aurora to be opened by Lieutenant Governor

Aurora, ON, June 20, 2000 – A 'pathway for peace,' a fundraising initiative for women's shelter Yellow Brick House, will be officially opened in Aurora June 27 by the Honourable Hilary M. Weston, the Lieutenant Governor of Ontario.

The path has been built through the centre of Temperance Park, just west of Aurora's main intersection of Yonge and Wellington Streets. Individuals, families and companies can purchase bricks in the path to raise money for Yellow Brick House. All purchasers, and project donors, will have their names (or names of their choice) placed on a plaque that will be mounted on the monument in September.

Bricks are being sold for $25 (families and individuals), $100 (small business) and $1,000 (corporate). Contact Yellow Brick House at (905) 727-0930 Ext. 230 to purchase a brick.

Why: Path opening by the Honourable Hilary M. Weston, Lieutenant Governor of Ontario

When: Tuesday, June 27, 2000, 11 a.m.

Where: Temperance Park is located on the south side of Wellington Street West, at Temperance Street, one block west of Yonge Street. Aurora Town Hall is three lights east of Yonge and Wellington Streets on John West Way. Town Hall is one block north on the west side.

A public reception will follow at Aurora Town Hall after a brief private tour of Yellow Brick House. Her Honour will arrive at Town Hall at approximately 11:45 a.m.

For more information, please contact: *[Name, office phone, cell phone, and email addresses of PR, client, and third party if applicable]*

NEWS RELEASE

Pathway for Peace in Aurora opened by Lieutenant Governor

Aurora, ON, June 27, 2000 – A 'pathway for peace,' a fundraising initiative for women's shelter Yellow Brick House, was officially opened in Aurora today by the Honourable Hilary M. Weston, the Lieutenant Governor of Ontario.

The path has been built through the centre of Temperance Park, just west of Aurora's main intersection of Yonge and Wellington Streets. Individuals, families and companies can purchase bricks in the path to raise money for Yellow Brick House. All purchasers, and project donors, will have their names (or names of their choice) placed on a plaque that will be mounted on the monument in September.

Bricks are being sold for $25 (families and individuals), $100 (small business) and $1,000 (corporate). Contact Yellow Brick House at (905) 727-0930 Ext. 230 to purchase a brick.

Besides raising money and awareness, the path project is also an acknowledgement of the Town of Aurora and its resident's support throughout Yellow Brick House's 21 years. It is hoped the pathway for peace fundraising concept may be used by other women's shelters across the province, and even nationally, creating a nationwide pathway for peace.

Founded in 1978, and located in Aurora since 1982, Yellow Brick House is a 21-bed shelter for abused and homeless women and their children. It also operates an eight- apartment longer-term facility (called Reta's Place and also located in Aurora) and an outreach office and counselling centre in Thornhill. It serves York Region and provides shelter, counselling, and education services. Visit www.yellowbrickhouse.org. Media may access this information electronically, and download images after the event, at www.yellowbrickhouse.org/media.

-30-

For more information, please contact: *[Name, office phone, cell phone, and email addresses of PR, client, and third party if applicable]*

"I Knew Kolorkins Could Fly"
Kodak Canada 100th Anniversary
Case Study (2001)

Our major objective in creating the Kodak Kolorkins event was to generate news media coverage of Kodak Canada's 100th anniversary as well as to launch a new promotion involving Kodak's mini bean bag Kolorkins. Research indicated that corporate anniversaries do not generate widespread media interest. We decided to create an event that would gain media interest, and themed it after the iconic Thanksgiving episode of the popular sitcom *WKRP in Cincinnati.* (Even people who didn't watch the show in either first run or syndication are familiar with the famous "turkey drop" episode.) The event consisted of two helicopters dropping the Kolorkins with parachutes towards a giant "100" painted on Kodak's parking lot. Mayor Mel Lastman attended as a judge. Kodak employees donated $10,000 to a local homeless youth shelter. Mr. Lastman also declared our anniversary date as Kodak Centennial Day and Kodak Photo Week. Nineteen news media attended, generating television coverage on every GTA television station as well as numerous print and Internet articles.

Objectives
- Generate news coverage on launching Kodak's Centennial initiatives.
- Generate news coverage of the launch of Kodak's mini-bean bag Kolorkins.
- Generate news coverage on the new Kodak DCS620 professional digital camera.
- Have Mayor declare Kodak Centennial Photo Day or Week.
- Provide an event to generate employee enthusiasm.

Research
- Primary and secondary research indicated that company anniversaries, even those as significant as centennials, have difficulty gaining media coverage in the Greater Toronto Area (GTA) media.
- Anecdotal research (brief media survey) determined that *WKRP* enjoys high recall among "media types."
- Transport Canada and helicopter specialists provided green light for tactical elements.

- Developed parachute to enable Kolorkins to safely descend from helicopter. Two test Kolorkin drops were carried out.
- Researched local charitable recipients that tied in with Kodak's philanthropic programs.

Strategy

Provided a significant photo opportunity for daily newspaper and television photojournalists and videographers at Kodak's Canadian headquarters and plant site.

News Hooks

- Kolorkin/Centennial launch
- 100 employees
- VIP as judge
- Charity as recipient
- Use of the new Kodak DCS620 (in helicopter)
- Webcast

Strategic Considerations

- VIP as judge: Mayor Mel Lastman agreed to officiate.
- Charity: identified as Horizons for Youth (a homeless youth shelter)—it was tied to the event to reduce the "commerciality" that some media may use as an excuse not to attend.
- Capitalized on the highly popular "As God is my witness I thought turkeys could fly" episode from the TV show *WKRP in Cincinnati*
- Timed event to take place in May, which was Photography Month
- The news media was at that time focused on helicopters as an aid to police chases throughout the GTA.

Event Elements/Tactics

- Two helicopters hired to drop 100 (in three batches) Kodak Kolorkins with parachutes onto Kodak's parking lot east of Building 11. Second helicopter flew above first helicopter to shoot the Kolorkins landing. This provided media with an additional photo angle, as well as the photo for the paid wire photo release and video for TV.
- Below the helicopter was a giant "100" (25 feet by 25 feet) painted in large numbers on the parking lot.
- The Kolorkin Parachutists were targeted at the two zeroes. The number to fall in the zeroes would determine the amount of money to

- be donated by Kodak to the designated charitable recipient ($10,000 would be awarded despite how many actually landed in the zeroes).
- Helicopter rides after the event were offered to assembled photojournalists and editors of photo specialty publications (i.e. Don Long, Gunter Ott) so they could use the new DCS620 professional digital camera to shoot the "100" focal point. Employees were also offered rides.
- Six DCS620's were made available to attending media.
- Media were invited to attend the event via a paid newswire (GTA only) media advisory. National media were invited with a webcast focus; hard copy of media advisory with an actual Kolorkin was distributed to photo editors/TV assignment editors directly three weeks prior. Follow up was conducted by telephone calls and email.
- A videographer was hired to record the event and distribute video to local TV stations (i.e. CFTO/City/Global). Also, a CNW 60-second report was created from that tape. A photojournalist was hired to shoot the event and move that image with cutline on paid newswire after the event to complement media coverage.
- Fencing assembled per Transport Canada regulations. Parking plan developed for 280 vehicles to fit around the cordoned-off area with the rest sent to back field.
- Tent (50 X100 feet) assembled with media table, podium, sound system, and Ethernet connection for live webcast. Refreshments inside tent. A live webcast was conducted from the tent.
- Kodak 100th anniversary collaterals developed (hats, pins, bookmarks, t-shirts, Kolorkins, and jackets worn by all participants) for employees and guests.
- Blown-up and real cheque for $10,000
- Two-way radios for key personnel (pilots, PR, Security).
- A 100-foot crane was reserved in case of high winds or severe weather.

Budget
[Client considers this proprietary.]

Evaluation: *Met Objectives*
- Nineteen media attended the event. Television coverage generated in all GTA television stations (video picked up by non-attending TV stations City-tv, CP24, and CFMT). Total of 13 TV broadcasts,

reaching 1.9 million viewers. Print coverage generated in key trades (for digital camera business) including front cover of *Computer Dealer News*. Coverage generated in *Adnews*, key trade for Kolorkin promotion. Total reach of 2.3 million readers.

- Webcast had more than 100,000 hits. Internet coverage of event reached more than 500,000 audience.
- Mayor Mel Lastman officially declared week of May 3 to 8 as Kodak Photo Week and May 6 as Kodak Centennial Day.
- Kodak internally described the event as "the best in its 100-year history."

Post-Mortem

- Although this was an event closed to the general public (because of safety concerns), the media advisory did not stipulate that fact so media reported it was happening the morning of. Copy should have stipulated.
- Although two GTA daily newspaper photographers did attend, those newspapers did not run coverage. The shot proved very difficult to perform both from the ground and air. A raised platform closer to the drop area may have helped, although safety requirements negated such a platform. More time aloft to get the perfect shot may have helped, but time constraints on the helicopter rental negated a time extension.
- More budget was needed to retain attendance of Toronto's Gordon Jump, *WKRP*'s Arthur Carlson.

MEDIA ADVISORY

As God is my witness, I thought Kolorkins could fly

A new breed of paratrooper will adorn the skies over Toronto May 6 to officially launch Kodak Canada's 100th Anniversary. More than 100 Mini Bean Bag Kolorkins, equipped with parachutes, will be dropped from a helicopter (Bell Long Ranger) hovering over Kodak Canada's Toronto plant.

The Mini Kolorkins will attempt to land within the zeroes of a giant "100" painted on the surface of the parking lot. Mayor Mel Lastman will judge how many will actually land within the zeros. For every successful Mini Kolorkin landing within the zeroes, $100 will be donated to the Horizons for Youth organization, a local shelter for homeless and troubled youth. The Mayor will also officially declare May 6 as Kodak Centennial Day.

A second helicopter (Robinson R44) will hover above the first to provide news photographers and videographers with another angle to shoot the parachute drop over the plant's main parking lot. As well, the new Kodak DCS620 professional and DC265 consumer digital cameras will be available to news media to shoot the event both from the air and ground.

The event will also be webcast on www.kodak.ca One hundred Kodak employees will also be on hand to officially witness the Kolorkin drop.

The four inch tall Mini Kolorkins are descendants of the popular 10-inch tall Kolorkins of the 1980s, and used by Kodak worldwide to act as ambassadors, mascots and premium items for the promotion of Kodak products. The series of five different Mini Kolorkins will be available to purchasers of Kodak products throughout the company's Centennial year of 1999.

When: Thursday, May 6, 1999 at 11 a.m.

Where: Kodak Canada's plant at Black Creek and Eglinton. Enter from the north side of the plant off Industry Street, which runs off Todd Bayliss Boulevard (off Black Creek, first light north of Eglinton on the west side of Black Creek).

Why: To launch Kodak Canada's 100th Anniversary with the Mini Kolorkins and the company's new DCS 620 professional digital camera.

For more information, please contact: *[Name, office phone, cell phone, and email addresses of PR, client, and third party if applicable]*

NEWS RELEASE

As God is my witness, I knew Kolorkins could fly

Toronto, ON, May 6, 1999 – More than one hundred Mini Bean Bag paratroopers landed on Kodak Canada's parking lot today to kick off the company's 100th anniversary in this country.

The four-inch tall Mini Bean Bag Kolorkins, descendants of the popular 10-inch tall Kolorkins of the 1980s, helped raise $10,000 for Horizons for Youth organization, a local shelter for homeless and troubled youth that is in the same neighbourhood of Kodak's sprawling plant.

The Mini Kolorkins will attempt to land within the zeroes of a giant "100" painted on the surface of the parking lot. Toronto Mayor Mel Lastman officiated as judge to determine how many Mini Kolorkins actually landed within the zeroes of a massive painted "100" on the surface of the company's parking lot. The Mini Kolorkins were dropped from a helicopter, hovering 100 feet above the parking lot. The Mayor also officially declared May 6 as Kodak Centennial Day.

"As God is my witness, I knew the Mini Kolorkins could fly," quipped Ted Knight, Director, Corporate and Business Unit Communications, Kodak Canada Inc. "We are very proud to have been in this country for 100 years," added Ed Jurus, President, Kodak Canada. "And we're looking forward to the next hundred."

Kodak Canada, which employs more than 1,400 people in Canada, manufactures a variety of products at its main Canadian facility, including inkjet and micrographic products for the worldwide market. The company's charter was officially issued November 3, 1899. Its first Canadian location was 41 Colborne Street in downtown Toronto.

Mayor Mel Lastman has earmarked the homeless issue as one of his main concerns as both mayor of the country's largest city and as a private citizen. He has successfully lobbied provincial and federal politicians to launch a number of initiatives on this issue.

Horizons for Youth organization is an emergency shelter for homeless and troubled youth aged 16 to 24. The shelter can provide 35 beds at any given time, and serves up to 800 young people each year. It is a member of the United Way.

Images, shot with the company's new DSC620 professional digital camera from a second helicopter, which hovered above the first, are available at

Kodak Canada's web site at www.kodak.ca/go/netcast. The series of five different Mini Kolorkins will be available to purchasers of Kodak products throughout the company's Centennial year of 1999.

For more information, please contact: *[Name, office phone, cell phone, and email addresses of PR, client, and third party if applicable]*

McCormick Gourmet Super Spices Case Study

Preamble

The Gourmet Super Spices campaign launched Tuesday, March 2, 2010. Media relations tactics included an English and French matte article package with article, sidebar, and recipes distributed via News Canada, English and French news releases distributed via Marketwire and direct email, and a Chinese news release distributed via Dynasty PR. Product sample kits went to an A-list of about 100 media.

PR Objectives

Through proactive product media relations, generate positive media coverage in both the consumer and trade food news holes to help drive awareness and sales. At least 10 million total impressions will be generated, a 75 per cent overall score (MRP) with a cost per contact of $0.05 or below.

Target Audiences

- Primary purchaser is female aged 35–54 with 2+ kids at home. Children under 18 at home, predominantly maturing (kids 6–12) and established (kids 13–17) families
- Relatively affluent households with income of $70M+
- Health focused homes

Target Markets

- Toronto (extended Golden Horseshoe): 6.6 million, including Peterborough, Kingston, Barrie, London, Guelph, Kitchener, Windsor, Ottawa, Hamilton
- Montreal, Quebec City (Laurentians/eastern townships) corridor: 3.6 million
- Vancouver and lower BC mainland including Whistler: 2.6 million
- Calgary/Edmonton Corridor: 1.9 million
- Maritimes: Halifax (NS), St. John's (NL): 500,000
- Prairies: Winnipeg, Saskatoon, Regina: 250,000
- Smaller towns and cities in between covered by News Canada distribution
- Chinese Canada focused in major urban areas including Vancouver, Calgary, Edmonton, Toronto and Montreal

Target Media

- Major-market daily newspapers and wire service contacts (mainstream food)
- Consumer magazines (mainly women targeted, food editors and writers)
- Trades and business magazines (food, packaging, grocery)
- Electronic media (radio and TV where relevant)
- Websites/ezines (food)
- Freelancers (mainly food)
- Community newspapers and small dailies (through News Canada distribution channel)

Strategic Considerations

Gourmet launch (September 13, 2007) generated a total reach of 30,429,472, with a cost per contact of $0.002 and an MRP score of 79 per cent.

Budget

Fees of $8,000 and disbursements of $15,890 for a total of $23,890.

Results

- Total impressions captured: 47,444,820 (10 million was target)
- Cost per impression: $0.001 ($0.05 was target)
- MRP 87.28 per cent (75 per cent target)

Highlights included the unusual pick-up by Rita Demontis of our Super Spices story in her nationally syndicated Eat column, netting in verbatim coverage sourced from her *Toronto Sun* full page article in 30 Sun Media dailies and 28 online corresponding properties. Major daily pick-up here included the Toronto, Winnipeg, Ottawa, Edmonton, and Calgary *Suns*. Total impressions there were 5.3 million impressions. Other major news portals in English and French that picked up the story in verbatim fashion from the news release included Yahoo, Google, Alta Vista, Reuters, Congoo, Findarticles, Topix, MSNBC with reviews in Tidingsmag.com, *Canadian Packaging, 24 Heures, Hamilton Spectator, Grocer Today, Ontario Restaurant News, Pacific/Prairie Restaurant News*. Total impressions there were 31.7 million impressions. News Canada-distributed articles and recipes netted 8.1 million impressions, with Chinese media relations brining in 1.8 million impressions.

NEWS RELEASE

McCormick Gourmet Super Spices: A new reason to season

London, ON, March 2, 2010 – Nutritionists have long recommended spices and herbs as a way to add flavour without fat, salt or sugar—making it easier to meet today's dietary guidelines. But now studies suggest adding more spices and herbs to your diet may not only please your palate, it could enhance your health.

"To make it easy and delicious to enjoy the potential benefits of spices, we have created a unique collection of new recipes, specially designed to deliver up to half a teaspoon of antioxidant-rich spices per serving," says Brian Rainey, Executive Vice-President Sales & Marketing for McCormick Canada. "Many spices and herbs appear to have some beneficial effects, but there are 10 McCormick Gourmet Super Spices that may hold the greatest potential to improve our health."

McCormick Gourmet 10 Super Spices:

- Cinnamon
- Ginger
- Oregano
- Paprika
- Cayenne Pepper
- Parsley
- Basil
- Rosemary
- Thyme
- Turmeric *(common in curry powder)*

Botanically, spices and herbs are classified as fruits and vegetables. That's why these plant-derived ingredients are naturally high in antioxidants. And, since they no longer contain the water that makes up a significant part of the weight of fresh produce, spices and herbs offer a big antioxidant punch in a very compact package.

Spices and herbs also are rich in phytonutrients, such as carotenoids, flavonoids and other phenolics, which possess health-promoting properties beyond being great antioxidants.

To help enjoy the taste and health benefits of these 10 McCormick Gourmet Super Spices throughout the course of the day, here are some simple tips:

At breakfast:

- Sprinkle Cinnamon on your bowl of oatmeal, yogurt, French toast or muffin batter.
- A dash of Thyme is a welcome addition to scrambled eggs or omelettes.

At lunch:

- Stir dried Oregano Leaves or Crushed Red Pepper Flakes into favourite canned soups, chicken/tuna salads or vinaigrette dressings. Try these on pizza to get a delicious antioxidant boost.
- A sprinkling of Ground Ginger over sliced fresh fruit makes a refreshing dessert.

At dinner:

- Wake up the flavours of favourite side dishes with Crushed Rosemary Leaves (a natural with mashed or roasted potatoes) or Curry Powder (perfect for rice dishes or couscous.)

More information and recipes can be found at www.spicesforhealth.ca.

McCormick Canada is a wholly-owned subsidiary of McCormick & Company, Inc., a global leader in the manufacture, marketing and distribution of spices, seasonings and flavours to the entire food industry. Founded in 1889 in Baltimore, Maryland, McCormick & Company employs more than 7,500 people. McCormick & Company includes Schwartz (UK), McCormick Foods Australia, Ducros (France), McCormick de Centro América (Central America), and AVT McCormick (India). McCormick Canada celebrated its 125th anniversary in 2008. More information can be found at www.mccormick.com.

Product and recipe photos are parked at: www.marketwire.com/mccormick.

To view directions/ingredients/tips for the Mango-Blueberry Cobbler and Citrus Salmon with Orange Relish recipes, please visit the following link: **http://media3.marketwire.com/docs/McCormickGourmetSpicesforHealthNewsRelease.doc.**

For news media information and product samples, please contact: *[Name, office phone, cell phone, and email addresses of PR, client, and third party if applicable]*

SANYO Internet Radio Case Study

Product Synopsis

The SANYO Internet Radio R227 with built-in Wi-Fi provides an easy to use Internet audio interface that plays thousands of free stations from around the world without a subscription. Perfect for the bedroom, den, kitchen, office, or even hotel room, the Sanyo Internet Radio sports an easy network key entry when used on secured wireless networks. It enables search by country or genre, with eight Internet station presets. It also has an FM stereo digital tuner with eight station presets. Loaded with clock radio functionality, including wake-to-internet or FM radio, the R227 boasts excellent stereo audio with dual speakers. A simple one-button on/off negates complex computer boot-up, player selection and shutdown issues, as well as provides easy background audio while working on a computer without overloading Internet feeds. It also solves the problem of poor AM reception in many offices and condominiums by accessing an AM station's web stream instead. The unit is quite compact at 215 X 140 X 110 mm/8.6 X 5.6 X 4.4 inches (wxhxd). Complete with remote control, built-in Wi-Fi, Ethernet jack and input jacks for MP3/WMA players, audio-out and stereo headphone jacks, the R227 will be available in Canada by November, 2008. It supports such audio files as AAC, AIFF, MP3, RM, WAV, WMA and playlists (M3V) stored on a networked computer. It will be initially marketed in a black wood gloss finish and brushed aluminum front through selected retailers for an MSRP of $219.99.

Planning began in December, 2007, with launch October 27, 2008.

Objectives

- To generate significant early adopter news media buzz for this product.
- To generate minimum of 10 million impressions, with a cost per contact of at least $0.005.

Strategic Considerations

- Sanyo's first major mainstream audio product was its transistor radio in 1956.
- Canada is one of the leading countries for both Internet use and Wi-Fi within offices and households.
- Canada has among the highest multicultural mix in the world, with

Toronto, Montreal and Vancouver being amongst the most multicultural cities.
- Canada has a plethora of news media serving this multicultural mix, including radio.

Target Audiences
- Tech adopters in 30- to 40-year-old age demographic, male skewed
- New Canadians
- Room guests at the more innovative or upscale hotels

Target Markets
- Extended Golden Horseshoe: 6.6 million, including Ottawa, Peterborough, Kingston, Barrie, London, Guelph, Kitchener, Windsor
- Calgary/Edmonton Corridor: 1.9 million
- Vancouver and lower BC mainland including Whistler: 2.6 million
- Maritimes

Tactics
- Three day exclusive to 680 News tied in with give-away promotion (October 23)
- Sanyo Canada launch October 27, worldwide exclusive (Sanyo US launch December 2, 2008)
- Paid wire distribution with photo as part of Marketwire/CP Press Pack
- Canadian Press photo shoot with product and model with product shots. CP photographer Dave Starrett captured beautiful generic downtown image in background as directed.
- Product loaner program—all products then purchased by media
- Chinese and South Asian media relations conducted by Dynasty Advertising and Public Relations, Markham, ON. Adaptation from English media materials

Results
- Total media outlets: 259
- Total hard copy: 54
- Total .com: 202
- Number of CP photo pick-ups: 131
- Total captured MRP impressions: 64,724,939
- Fees: $10,587.79

- Disbursements: $5,600.00
- Total: $16,187.79
- Cost per impression: $0.001
- MRP: 81.55 per cent
- Ad Value: $620,263.27

NEWS RELEASE

Sanyo Canada launches new Internet Radio product

Concord, ON, October 27, 2008 – Fifty-two years after it launched one of the world's first transistor radios, SANYO has unveiled in Canada its new Internet Radio, combining the convenience of Internet radio's plethora of crystal clear channels from around the world with wireless Internet efficacy.

The SANYO Internet Radio R227 with built-in Wi-Fi provides an easy to use Internet audio interface that plays thousands of stations and podcasts from around the world without a subscription fee.

High resolution product images are available at www.marketwire.com/sanyo/.

Perfect for the bedroom, den, kitchen, office, even a hotel room, the Sanyo Internet Radio sports an easy network key entry when used on secured wireless networks. It enables search by country or genre, with eight Internet station presets. It also has an FM stereo digital tuner with eight station presets.

"Canada is one of the most multicultural and urban concentrated countries in the world, and the SANYO Internet Radio R227 meets the needs of those radio aficionados perfectly," says Barry Richler, Vice President, Consumer Products, Sanyo Canada. "Many radio stations in remote parts of the world cannot be consistently received on conventional shortwave radios. Also, it is difficult to receive AM signals in many downtown offices and condominiums. The problem is easily solved by accessing a station's web stream instead," adds this industry veteran. "As well, you can listen to the eclectic music programming of such FM stations as WFUV out of New York City, or CKUA from Calgary, without having to turn on your computer, or sit at your desk for that matter. It will make you fall in love with radio all over again."

Loaded with clock radio functionality, including wake-to-internet or FM radio, the R227 boasts excellent stereo audio with dual speakers. A simple one-button on/off negates complex computer boot-up, player selection and shutdown issues, as well as provides easy background audio while working on a computer without having to reboot after those too-frequent updates from software providers.

The unit is quite compact at 215 X 140 X 110 mm/8.6 X 5.6 X 4.4 inches (wxhxd). Complete with remote control, built-in Wi-Fi, Ethernet socket, input for MP3/WMA players, headphone jack, and output to connect to an external audio system, the R227 will be available in Canada by late October, 2008. It supports such audio files as AAC, AIFF, MP3, RM, WAV, WMA and playlists (M3V) stored on a networked computer. It will be initially marketed in a black wood gloss finish through selected retailers for a very affordable MSRP of $219.99.*

SANYO Canada, established in 1958, is based in Concord, Ontario (a business suburb north of Toronto). Founded in 1947 in Osaka, Japan, SANYO, which stands for "three oceans," has $22 billion worldwide in sales. The company provides a full range of SANYO consumer and industrial products including audio and video, digital cameras, wireless communication, LCD projectors and monitors, security video, air conditioning and home appliance products. SANYO is also the world's largest manufacturer of rechargeable batteries. Its environmental focus includes solar energy panel products, non-fluorocarbon refrigeration, and electric vehicle power solutions (for the Ford Escape Hybrid and Honda Accord). It is also a major manufacturer of lab equipment and CO_2 incubators. Visit www.sanyo.ca for more information.

High resolution product images are available at www.marketwire.com/sanyo.

-30-

For news media information and information about loaners, please contact: *[Name, office phone, cell phone, and email addresses of PR, client, and third party if applicable]*

*Retailers may sell for less.

Canadian Canoe Pilgrimage Case Study
(Winner, CPRS Toronto ACE Awards: Silver, Media Relations, 2018;
Winner, CPRS National Awards: Bronze, Media Relations, 2019)

Preamble

In 1967, 24 Jesuits paddled in canoes from Martyrs' Shrine near Midland, Ontario to Expo 67 in Montreal, a distance of 850 kilometres. It took 21 days. By map, an exact repeat journey, with a core group of 30 paddlers (about one-third Jesuits, one-third Indigenous, and one-third lay collaborators), was successfully completed in July and August 2017, but this time continuing the work of the Truth and Reconciliation Commission. Also celebrating Canada's 150th birthday, it took 25 days.

Objectives

- Continuing the work of Canada's Truth and Reconciliation Commission (TRC) by fostering a community of paddlers comprised of Indigenous Peoples, Jesuits, English and French Canadians, young and old, male and female.
- Fundraising for the Canadian Canoe Pilgrimage (CCP) as well as for apostolates of the Jesuits in English Canada.
- Raising awareness of the Jesuits' significant role in the founding of Canada.
- Increasing awareness of the Jesuits for those discerning a vocation either to religious life or in support one of the Jesuits' apostolates in Canada.
- Through proactive media relations, generating positive media coverage in both the consumer and trade food news holes to help drive awareness and sales. At least 10 million total impressions will be generated, utilizing the MRP measurement system with a cost per contact of $0.05 or below.

Target Media

- Internet news providers via paid wire distribution
- Community newspapers and radio and TV stations along the route
- Mayors/MPPs/MPs were sent letters and media advisories relevant to route
- National media, such as the CBC
- Facebook with less focus on Twitter and Instagram
- Jesuit- and Catholic-oriented media

Target Markets

- Midland/Barrie/Orillia: Launch Mass and event from Saint Marie Park, July 21
- French River/Sudbury/North Bay: Special event at FR Visitor's Centre, July 28
- North Bay: Special event at Sisters of St. Joseph Motherhouse, July 31
- Mattawa: Special dinner at St. Anne's Parish, August 2
- Pembroke: Special event at Sisters of St. Joseph, August 6
- Ottawa: Special event at Royal Ottawa Golf Club, August 10
- Montreal: Special landing event at Villa St. Martin, August 14
- Kahnawà:ke: Final landing, August 15

Stakeholders

- The Jesuits in English and French Canada, as well as Jesuits within the Canada-US Jesuit Conference
- Indigenous peoples of Canada
- Local parishes along the route
- Young adults
- Federal, provincial, regional and municipal governments
- Media partners

Strategy

Utilized the local media angle of the pilgrimage moving through various locations to build a national story as well as springboard key messaging per the continuation of the Truth and Reconciliation Commission's Calls-to-Action.

Tactics

- Paid wire (Meltwater) was utilized for the initial news release three months prior to launch and for the launch media advisory.
- Media advisories were distributed in advance of each major media event including those for the French River landing, and for events in North Bay, Mattawa, Pembroke, Ottawa, and Montreal.
- Social media was utilized, including a Facebook page, Twitter and Instagram feeds.
- A wrap-up news release was distributed upon the successful final landing at Kahnawà:ke.
- Embedded videography and photography with the entire trip, which

was heavily utilized by media for stories, with a vast amount of imaging collected for a post-trip documentary.

Key Messages

Mission Statement: "Paddling Together"

The Canadian Canoe Pilgrimage brings together different cultures that form the fabric of Canada today. The pilgrimage will provide an experience of encounter that will encourage dialogue, reconciliation and friendship. We are immersed in the Calls-to-Action outlined in the Truth and Reconciliation Commission. Our vehicle for this encounter is a canoe pilgrimage spanning 25 days and 850 kilometres along a traditional water trade route with paddlers from Indigenous communities, Jesuits, English and French Canadians, men and women, young and old.

Primary Messaging

1) To bring different cultures together …

Canada is a mosaic. We are at our best when we celebrate and encourage diversity as well as grow in our understanding and appreciation of different cultures and traditions. Simply being with the other and experiencing together fuels this learning.

2) To encourage the skills needed for dialogue, reconciliation, and relationship building …

Our society is becoming increasingly polarized. The skills needed to combat this division are dialogue and active listening, trusting and respecting the other's viewpoint, and developing the capacity to share our own vulnerabilities.

3) To increase awareness around Canada's Truth and Reconciliation Commission and its Calls-to-Action …

The TRC's Calls-to-Action require immediate and active participation in order to acknowledge past and change current injustices faced by the Indigenous Peoples in Canada. It is this active participation that leads to trust and relationship building which are necessary for reconciliation.

4) To build on our rich and varied traditions …

Our various traditions are rich sources of wisdom. We must better understand these teachings of our ancestors in order that their richness can be shared for generations to come.

5) To foster a deeper respect, immersion and connection with all of creation around us ...

We are living in an ecological crisis. Scientists and some government leaders are stressing the need for immediate change. Pope Francis and other leaders, in solidarity with Indigenous Peoples (who have always valued living in harmony with creation), stress the urgency for personal and communal conversion.

PR Team

- Mark Hunter LaVigne, MA, APR, FCPRS (PR Director, Agency/Consultant)
- Erica Zlomislic (Communications Officer, Jesuits English Canada
- Adam Pittman, SJ (PR Logistics Embedded)
- Marco Veilleux (Communications Officer, Jesuits French Canada, Montreal Event)

Spokespersons

- Erik Sorensen, SJ (Embedded Key Jesuit and trip spokesperson, Trip Director)
- Kevin Kelly, SJ (Back-up Spokesperson, Coordinator, Logistics and fundraising)
- Paul Jacques (Embedded Navigator, Indigenous Spokesperson)

Videography/Photography

- Tim Wilson (Director)
- Eric Miller (Embedded videography)
- Dominik Haake (Embedded photography)

PR Advisers

- Ian Ross, APR
- Daniel Granger, LLB, MBA, APR, FCPRS
- Pierrette Leonard, APR, FCPRS

Results

- Total impressions: 43,546,773
- Total # of stories: 180
- Total # stories English: 137
- Total # stories French: 43
- Total stories print/online: 86

- Total stories broadcast: 94
- Total Fees: $59,325
- Total Disbursements: $7,700
- Total Fees/disbursements: $67,025
- Total cost per impression: .0015
- MRP score: 90.81 per cent

Media Highlights

- CBC.ca promo of *National* documentary
- 11-minute documentary on CBC's *The National* on Labour Day, 2017
- APTN National

Front Pages

- *Midland Mirror*
- *Orillia Packet and Times*
- *North Bay Nugget*
- *Pembroke Daily Observer*

ARTICLE FOR POSSIBLE MEDIA USE

[NOTE: The following article is written in such a way that it could be run as it stands by a media outlet (most likely a community newspaper). Such articles are sometimes still called "matte articles" from the days when they were produced in printer-ready hard-copy format; a community newspaper could simply include them in its formatted pages "as is" without having to typeset them again.]

Young people paddle hundreds of kilometres this summer, working toward reconciliation with Indigenous Peoples

More than 30 people, comprised of Indigenous, Jesuit, English and French Canadian paddlers, will embark on a month-long, 850-kilometre canoe trip July 21 in response to the Calls to Action of the Truth and Reconciliation Commission.

Following a traditional First Nations canoe trade route, the Canadian Canoe Pilgrimage (CCP) will begin at Midland, Ontario up Georgian Bay, travel across the French River, Lake Nipissing, the Mattawa and Ottawa Rivers, and end near Montreal.

"We are retracing this historic route on the 150th anniversary of Canada as a nation, but more importantly we are trying to work for reconciliation," says Erik Sorensen, SJ, Project Manager of the CCP. "As a member of the Jesuits, a group that had a residential school that played an integral role in colonization efforts by early Europeans, there is a collective healing that I am participating in. And we are changing the way we do things."

"I am hoping to learn a lot about the cultures that are going to be there," says Andrew Starblanket, who is Nēhiyaw and will be representing the Starblanket First Nation in Saskatchewan on the trip. "I guarantee that I'm going to learn a lot about myself and others."

"Ontario's 150th anniversary is an opportunity for us all to reflect on who we are and what we hope to be," said Eleanor McMahon, Minister of Tourism, Culture and Sport. "The Canadian Canoe Pilgrimage will give people the chance to connect with a meaningful part of our history, experience our province's breathtaking scenery firsthand, and contemplate all that we can achieve by working together."

Jesuit Pope Francis promotes a "culture of encounter," a culture where we engage others where they are at, offer welcome and hospitality, and are moved with compassion and the desire to treat all people with dignity. "This encounter is not about anything so specifically active, it's much more about just being with each other, across our respective cultures and traditions," says Kevin Kelly, SJ, a CCP co-organizer. "Encountering each other is about being ourselves and being open. This immersion experience into nature will also help participants increase their understanding of the current ecological crisis we face, especially the importance of water and our respect for and treatment of it."

The CCP tentative itinerary below shows major landfalls, but please be advised there may be changes due to logistical considerations and weather-related contingencies.

July 21: Departs Sainte-Marie among the Hurons (Midland, ON)
July 28: French River Provincial Park Visitor's Centre
July 31: North Bay, ON
August 2: Mattawa, ON
August 3: Deux Rivieres, ON
August 4: Stonecliffe, ON
August 5: Deep River, ON
August 6: Pembroke, ON
August 7: Portage-du-Fort, QC
August 8: Arnprior, ON
August 9/10: Ottawa, ON
August 11: Thurso, QC
August 12: Hawkesbury, ON
August 13: Hudson, QC
August 14: Montreal, Quebec
August 15: Kahnawà:ke First Nation (close to Montreal)

Members of the public will be able to join the CCP at special events at major stops along the route.

The Canadian Canoe Pilgrimage has been made possible by the generosity of donors including The Miller Group, the Ontario 150 Community Celebration Fund, the Canadian Heritage River System, Parks Canada, and Ontario Parks. Also thanks to Sainte-Marie among the Hurons and Martyrs' Shrine for hosting the launch event on July 21.

The Canadian Canoe Pilgrimage (CCP) is a project inspired by Canada's Truth and Reconciliation Commission (TRC) with the hope of encouraging intercultural and interreligious dialogue and learning. Participants, both Indigenous and non-Indigenous, will be immersed in each other's customs and traditions. Through this immersion, the goal is to foster deep respect, trust, dialogue and hopefully friendship, the building blocks for reconciliation.

The canoe route is a traditional First Nations trading route that was travelled by early European settlers such as Samuel de Champlain and Jean de Brébeuf, who were welcomed and guided by the Indigenous Peoples of this land. The route follows a similar one paddled by 24 young Jesuits in 1967. For more information, and to donate, please go to: www.canoepilgrimage.com.

-30-

NEWS RELEASE

Young people paddle hundreds of kilometres this summer, working toward reconciliation with Indigenous Peoples

Toronto, ON, April 20, 2017 – More than 30 people, comprised of Indigenous, Jesuit, English and French Canadian paddlers, will embark on a month-long, 850-kilometre canoe trip July 21 in response to the Calls to Action of the Truth and Reconciliation Commission.

Following a traditional First Nations canoe trade route, the Canadian Canoe Pilgrimage (CCP) will begin at Midland, Ontario up Georgian Bay, travel across the French River, Lake Nipissing, the Mattawa and Ottawa Rivers, and end near Montreal.

"We are retracing this historic route on the 150th anniversary of Canada as a nation, but more importantly we are trying to work for reconciliation," says Erik Sorensen, SJ, Project Manager of the CCP. "As a member of the Jesuits, a group that had a residential school that played an integral role in colonization efforts by early Europeans, there is a collective healing that I am participating in. And we are changing the way we do things."

"I am hoping to learn a lot about the cultures that are going to be there," says Andrew Starblanket, who is Nēhiyaw and will be representing the Starblanket First Nation in Saskatchewan on the trip. "I guarantee that I'm going to learn a lot about myself and others."

"Ontario's 150th anniversary is an opportunity for us all to reflect on who we are and what we hope to be," said Eleanor McMahon, Minister of Tourism, Culture and Sport. "The Canadian Canoe Pilgrimage will give people the chance to connect with a meaningful part of our history, experience our province's breathtaking scenery firsthand, and contemplate all that we can achieve by working together."

Jesuit Pope Francis promotes a "culture of encounter," a culture where we engage others where they are at, offer welcome and hospitality, and are moved with compassion and the desire to treat all people with dignity. "This encounter is not about anything so specifically active, it's much more about just being with each other, across our respective cultures and traditions," says Kevin Kelly, SJ, a CCP co-organizer. "Encountering each other is about being ourselves and being open. This immersion experience into nature will also help participants increase their understanding of the current ecological crisis we face, especially the importance of water and our respect for and treatment of it."

The CCP tentative itinerary below, shows major landfalls, but please be advised there may be changes due to logistical considerations and weather related contingencies.

July 21:   Departs Sainte-Marie among the Hurons (Midland, ON)
July 31:   North Bay, ON
August 2:   Mattawa, ON
August 6:   Pembroke, ON
August 9:   Ottawa, ON
August 14: Montreal, Quebec
August 15: Kahnawà:ke First Nation (close to Montreal)

Members of the public will be able to join the CCP at special events at major stops along the route.

The Canadian Canoe Pilgrimage has been made possible by the generosity of donors including The Miller Group, the Ontario 150 Community Celebration Fund, the Canadian Heritage River System, Parks Canada, and Ontario Parks. Also thanks to Sainte-Marie among the Hurons and Martyrs' Shrine for hosting the launch event on July 21.

About the Canadian Canoe Pilgrimage
The Canadian Canoe Pilgrimage (CCP) is a project inspired by Canada's Truth and Reconciliation Commission (TRC) with the hope of encouraging intercultural and interreligious dialogue and learning. Participants, both Indigenous and non-Indigenous, will be immersed in each other's customs and traditions. Through this immersion, the goal is to foster deep respect, trust, dialogue and hopefully friendship, the building blocks for reconciliation.

The canoe route is a traditional First Nations trading route that was travelled by early European settlers such as Samuel de Champlain and Jean de Brébeuf, who were welcomed and guided by the Indigenous Peoples of this land. This pilgrimage will begin at Sainte-Marie among the Hurons in Midland, on the shore of Georgian Bay, on July 21 and end on August 15 on the St. Lawrence River at the Kahnawake First Nation, close to Montreal. The community of paddlers making this 850-kilometre, 25-day voyage is comprised of Indigenous Peoples, Jesuits, English and French Canadians, men and women—all desiring to travel together on a path of healing and friendship. The route follows a similar one paddled by 24 young Jesuits in 1967. For more information, and to donate, please go to: www.canoepilgrimage.com.

About the Jesuits in English Canada
The Jesuits, an order of priests and brothers in the Roman Catholic Church, have worked in Canada for more than 400 years. They have responsibil-

ity for the direction of schools, churches, retreat houses, and a variety of social justice ministries that span from St. John's, Newfoundland and Labrador to Vancouver, British Columbia. They have worked closely with the TRC and issued a public Statement of Reconciliation in 2013. The Jesuits are currently implementing the Calls to Action described by the TRC. For more details please visit www.jesuits.ca.

For news media information and government please contact: *[Name, office phone, cell phone, and email addresses of PR, client, and third party if applicable]*

MEDIA ADVISORY

Young people leave Midland July 21 to paddle hundreds of kilometres, working toward reconciliation with Indigenous Peoples

Toronto, ON, July 11, 2017 – More than 30 people, comprised of Indigenous, Jesuit, English and French Canadian paddlers leave Midland on July 21 at 12:00 noon for a month-long, 850-kilometre canoe trip in response to the Calls to Action of the Truth and Reconciliation Commission.

By helping both Indigenous and non-Indigenous to be immersed in each other's customs and traditions for an entire month, the Canadian Canoe Pilgrimage (CCP) hopes to foster respect, trust, dialogue and hopefully friendships—the building blocks for reconciliation.

Following a traditional First Nations canoe trade route, the CCP will begin at Midland, Ontario then go up Georgian Bay, travel across the French River, Lake Nipissing, the Mattawa and Ottawa Rivers, and end near Montreal.

Who: Father Peter Bisson, SJ (Provincial, Jesuits in English Canada), William Baird (General Manager, Sainte-Marie among the Hurons), Father Michael Knox, SJ (Director, Martyrs' Shrine), Gerry Marshall (Warden, County of Simcoe and Mayor, Town of Penetanguishene), Gord McKay (Mayor of Midland), Scott Warnock (Mayor of Tay Township).

What: Launch of the Canadian Canoe Pilgrimage, an 850-kilometre canoe trip in response to the Calls to Action of the Truth and Reconciliation Commission.

When: Friday, July 21, launch ceremonies begin at 12 noon, a Mass precedes the send-off at 10:30 AM. Reception at 1:30 PM in Ste. Marie's restaurant.

Where: Launch is from Sainte-Marie Park, located off Wye Valley Road, adjacent to the bridge on Hwy. 12, over the Wye River, between Martyrs' Shrine and Sainte-Marie among the Hurons, 16164 Highway #12, Midland.

The CCP itinerary below shows major landfalls, but please be advised there may be changes due to logistical considerations and weather-related contingencies.

July 21 – Departs Sainte-Marie among the Hurons (Midland, ON)
July 28 – French River Visitor's Centre, French River Provincial Park

July 31 – North Bay, ON
August 2 – Mattawa, ON
August 6 – Pembroke, ON
August 9 – Ottawa, ON
August 14 – Montreal, Quebec
August 15 – Kahnawà:ke First Nation (close to Montreal)

For photos, video and news releases, please go to: https://canoepilgrimage.com/2017/04/20/press-release/

The Canadian Canoe Pilgrimage has been made possible by the generosity of donors including The Miller Group, the Ontario 150 Community Celebration Fund, the Canadian Heritage River System, Parks Canada, and Ontario Parks. Also thanks to Sainte-Marie among the Hurons and Martyrs' Shrine for hosting the launch event on July 21.

About the Canadian Canoe Pilgrimage
The Canadian Canoe Pilgrimage (CCP) is a project inspired by Canada's Truth and Reconciliation Commission (TRC) with the hope of encouraging intercultural and interreligious dialogue and learning. Participants, both Indigenous and non-Indigenous, will be immersed in each other's customs and traditions. Through this immersion, the goal is to foster respect, trust, dialogue and hopefully friendship—the building blocks for reconciliation.

The canoe route is a traditional First Nations trading route that was travelled by early European settlers such as Samuel de Champlain and Jean de Brébeuf, who were welcomed and guided by the Indigenous Peoples of this land. This pilgrimage will begin at Sainte-Marie among the Hurons in Midland, on the shore of Georgian Bay, on July 21 and end on August 15 on the St. Lawrence River at the Kahnawake First Nation, close to Montreal. The community of paddlers making this 850-kilometre, 25-day voyage is comprised of Indigenous Peoples, Jesuits, English and French Canadians, men and women—all desiring to travel together on a path of healing and friendship. The route follows a similar one paddled by 24 young Jesuits in 1967. For more information, and to donate, please go to: www.canoepilgrimage.com.

About the Jesuits in English Canada
The Jesuits, an order of priests and brothers in the Roman Catholic Church, have worked in Canada for more than 400 years. They have responsibility for the direction of schools, churches, retreat houses, and a variety of social justice ministries that span from St. John's, Newfoundland and Labrador to Vancouver, British Columbia. They have worked closely with the TRC and issued a public Statement of Reconciliation in 2013. The Jesuits

are currently implementing the Calls to Action described by the TRC. For more details please visit www.jesuits.ca.

About Sainte-Marie among the Hurons
Ontario's first European Community, Sainte-Marie among the Hurons was the headquarters for the French Jesuit Mission to the Huron Wendat people. In 1639, the Jesuits, along with French lay workers, began construction of a fenced community that included barracks, a church, workshops, residences, and a sheltered area for Native visitors. By 1648, Sainte-Marie was a wilderness home to 66 French men, representing one-fifth of the entire population of New France. Sainte-Marie's brief history ended in 1649, when members of the mission community were forced to abandon and burn their home of nearly ten years. After extensive archaeological and historical research, Sainte-Marie among the Hurons is now recreated on its original site, where the mission's compelling story is brought to life. More information may be found at http://www.saintemarieamongthehurons.on.ca.

About Martyrs' Shrine
Martyrs' Shrine is the National Shrine to the Canadian martyrs, celebrating its 90th season, and is a ministry of the Jesuits in English Canada. This house of prayer and home of peace honours the Jesuit missionaries and their companions who lived, worked, and died here more than 350 years ago. It is located in Midland, Ontario, in the heart of the Huron Confederacy of the 17th century. More than 110,000 visitors from around the world and from all cultural backgrounds are welcomed to the Shrine's 75-acre landscaped grounds each year. More information may be found at: http://martyrs-shrine.com.

NEWS RELEASE

Paddlers complete month-long 850-km reconciliation canoe pilgrimage at the Kahnawà:ke Mohawk Territory

Toronto, ON, August 21, 2017 – More than 30 individuals, Indigenous, Jesuit, English and French Canadian paddlers, have completed a 25-day, 850-kilometre canoeing expedition from Midland, Ontario to Montreal, Quebec in response to the Calls to Action of the Truth and Reconciliation Commission.

This pilgrimage has focused on deepening relationships with Indigenous and non-Indigenous People, while being immersed in each other's customs and traditions. The Canadian Canoe Pilgrimage (CCP) was successful in beginning a significant step forward in a process that has created an awareness around fostering respect, trust, dialogue and friendship: building blocks for reconciliation.

Following a traditional First Nations canoe trade route, the CCP began in Midland, Ontario on July 21, paddled up Georgian Bay, across the French River, Lake Nipissing, the Mattawa River and down the Ottawa River to Kahnawake First Nation close to Montreal.

"This trip was physically demanding, and we were exposed to all kinds of weather from fierce thunderstorms to blazing sun," says Erik Sorensen, 27, a Jesuit paddler and project manager for the CCP. "This pilgrimage has been about starting a process of reconciliation, and I believe we have been able to achieve this goal in simple ways, including many discussions by the fire, and sharing from elders."

Paul Jacques, 30, an Indigenous paddler from Northern Ontario says, "It was an honour to be the trip's navigator." He added, "I have made friends for life on this trip, learned new skills, and I am hopeful for the future."

The Canadian Canoe Pilgrimage continues to seek financial support, and is thankful for the many generous donors and benefactors. The Miller Group, the Ontario 150 Community Celebration Fund, the Canadian Heritage River System, Parks Canada, Ontario Parks, Jim Rook with the French River Delta Association, Mike Palmer with the Hartley Bay House Marina and numerous religious congregations and personal donors.

Also, the CCP expresses gratitude to the many communities that opened their doors to the group, especially Sainte-Marie among the Hurons, and Martyrs' Shrine in Midland, for hosting the launch event on July 21.

The CCP is still actively fundraising to pay for the journey. Please go to: https://www.canadahelps.org/dn/30907.

For photos, video and news releases, please go to: https://canoepilgrimage.com/news.

About the Canadian Canoe Pilgrimage
The Canadian Canoe Pilgrimage (CCP) is a project inspired by Canada's Truth and Reconciliation Commission (TRC) with the hope of encouraging intercultural and interreligious dialogue and learning. Participants, both Indigenous and non-Indigenous, will be immersed in each other's customs and traditions. Through this immersion, the goal is to foster respect, trust, dialogue and hopefully friendship—the building blocks for reconciliation.

The canoe route is a traditional First Nations trading route that was travelled by early European settlers such as Samuel de Champlain and Jean de Brébeuf, who were welcomed and guided by the Indigenous Peoples of this land. The route follows a similar one paddled by 24 young Jesuits in 1967. For more information, and to donate, please go to: www.canoepilgrimage.com.

About the Jesuits in English Canada
The Jesuits, an order of priests and brothers in the Roman Catholic Church, have worked in Canada for more than 400 years. They have responsibility for the direction of schools, churches, retreat houses, and a variety of social justice ministries that span from St. John's, Newfoundland and Labrador to Vancouver, British Columbia. They have worked closely with the TRC and issued a public Statement of Reconciliation in 2013. The Jesuits are currently implementing the Calls to Action described by the TRC. For more details please visit: www.jesuits.ca.

-30-

USB News Kits Hit Primetime

Face-to-face media interaction, whether in one-on-one interviews or at news events, requires a convenient way to provide the news gatherer with an easy-to-use and portable news kit.

Costs have fallen in the electronic news kit production area for USB sticks.

High-tech and electronics journalist Gordon Brockhouse, former editor of *Here's How* magazine, advises that a one-page hard copy news release accompany the USB stick so time-pressured news media can make a decision in five seconds whether or not to even load that media into their systems.

He also finds electronic news kits much easier to use than going to web sites looking for images, even when direct URLs are supplied. He recommends the hard copy news release accompanying the electronic news kit include a menu of what's actually on the USB stick, to speed up the news processing even further.

Electronic news kits become particularly useful at media events, or to send along with product shipments, whether hardware or software. Email media relations, if the above protocol is followed, is also very effective. Combining both is the best way to go, so key media are reached by two channels and invariably can at least find one of the communications under deadline pressure.

The time pressures journalists face are very important to keep in mind. Ipsos Reid, in their comprehensive media survey in 2005, found on average that business journalists receive about 150 news releases per week (about 18 per cent are used). They also get an average 19 news conference invitations per month, with about 50 per cent getting a reporter to attend. On average, 60 annual reports are received per year (16 per cent are used quickly). And 20 media kits are received per month (19 per cent are used).

Electronic News Dissemination Tips

- Embed the news release within the email message. Attachments are time consuming, and can be infected with a virus. Therefore, many journalists simply delete attachments.
- Format the embedded news release. Transferring from word processing software will always leave unsightly and hard-to-read aberrations. Take the time to correct those before hitting the send button.
- Blind-copy (BCC) your distribution. The number of contacts being targeted could easily take up a page or two before the copy starts. This will frustrate a journalist, who may very well hit the delete button in response. Also, you may not want to share all of your contacts with everybody (not to mention there may be privacy concerns).
- Use specific subject lines. Something like "Company XYZ news release" will simply get lost in the shuffle!
- Attempt to research beats properly so media are properly targeted.
- Include prices in the news release if it is product related, as most high tech news releases are. A lot of the freelancers work when many practitioners and clients are sleeping. Make sure the prices are in Canadian funds!
- Include a direct URL with the release so news media can quickly go to a section of the client's web site to retrieve high-resolution product images or other large files and/or lengthy works such as backgrounders, annual reports, and white papers.
- Include a technical contact with releases to help with installation or other problems.

Backgrounders and Position Papers

There are a number of media relations writing tactics and products that we will cover briefly in the following pages. Many of these can be effective elements for news media kits, electronic news kit compilations and web sites. We'll begin with brief descriptions of two quite similar items, the backgrounder and position paper.

The Backgrounder

The backgrounder looks in the rear-view mirror and creates context. There are several kinds:

- Problem/solution
- History of an organization
- History of a product: How made, where came from, process
- Company/organization or industry backgrounder
- Biography of a person
- Accomplishments

The Position Paper

A position paper is also known as a white paper or briefing notes and sometimes is confused with a backgrounder. But a position paper is forward-looking, while a backgrounder is backward-looking. In short, a position paper or white paper is a detailed report about an issue or trend relating to an organization or an industry.

A position paper can be used to brief spokespeople in advance of meeting various publics such as news media or investors. It can also be distributed to opinion leaders and news media to provide an organization's position on a particular issue (often tied to changes in regulations or laws).

The Do's and Don'ts of Writing Personality Profiles

- Do create a full picture.
- Do tell the reader who the subject is and why he or she is interesting.
- Do treat the profile as an interpretation, not necessarily an official biography.
- Do understand the subject's motivations.
- Don't write in chronological order. Start at why the subject is interesting *now*.
- Do ask the subject to reflect, evaluate himself or herself, and to describe good and bad points, highs and lows.
- Don't just focus on his or her job. Try to see the whole person. What does he or she do at home? What are his or her hobbies?
- Do describe the person. Are they serious, jovial, upbeat? What are they like under stress, at play, relaxed?
- Do keep in mind that personality profiles often can become the focus of a larger feature on an organization.
- Don't forget to look for the interesting hook.

Organizational Profiles

Sometimes personality and organizational profiles can blend, depending on which is the more interesting focus, the organization or the individual.

An organizational profile is similar to a fact sheet, but written in feature article style. It includes various facts about an organization: its objectives, main business activity, size, market position, revenues, products, and key executives. Much of this ends up as the boilerplate for a news release. Major anniversaries or changes in a business often lead to the creation of a historical corporate profile: "Thirty years ago, XYZ Corporation started in Larry's garage..."

Elements and Characteristics of a Feature Article

The format of a feature article is similar to that of a news release, providing contacts, headlines and datelines, but it is often used to generate coverage of softer news and to provide context or background.

Elements

- *Headline:* Informational or creative (play on words, puns, alliteration, rhymes).
- *Lead:* A news release lead is a summary of facts. A feature lead is much softer, and starts with the focus, which is intended to attract attention.
- *Body:* Can be as long as it takes to tell the story, up to 10 pages. However, the medium dictates the message. A food feature is often 500 to 750 words long. Business features can run between 1,000 and 2,000 words, entertainment pieces the same. Newspapers have less space, magazines more.
- *Summary:* News release summaries often include boilerplate. Feature summaries reinforce the crux of the story.

Characteristics

A picture paints a thousand words. A feature can provide the palette for that picture with:

- A soft sell approach—use the client or product name sparingly.
- Extensive use of quotes
- Colourful use of descriptive words, making a feature article entertaining to read

Features can be distributed and used in several ways:

- Distribute them to a variety of publications.
- Write an exclusive for one publication.
- Interest a freelancer or reporter in a story.
- Post on the organization's web site.
- Buy the space (advertorial).

Placement opportunities exist in:

- Specialty newspaper sections (auto, food, real estate)
- General or specialty magazines
- Business and trade magazines
- Internal publications
- E-zines and web sites

Public Service Announcements

Public service announcements (PSAs) are used heavily in radio, less so in television, and also in print, particularly in community events sections. Broadcasters like CBC and CTV as well as radio stations provide free air time for a certain number of public service announcements.

PSAs are used to promote programs run by non-profit organizations and government (but not election ads); sometimes informational programs from trade groups qualify.

Content should be tested by checking with a sample group of PSA directors at radio and TV.

PSAs generally air outside of prime time, but getting celebrities to act as spokespeople is invaluable in enabling a higher frequency of airings as well as scheduling during periods of peak exposure.

For radio and TV, PSAs should be scripted in UPPER CASE and double-spaced; they should vary in length (e.g., 60 seconds, 30 seconds, 15 seconds) to maximize flexibility in airing them. When recording them in video and/or audio form, MP3s and MPEG4s are fine. Web site addresses should be included.

If possible, make the content of scripts as local as possible to maximize interest.

The most highly used PSAs relate to kids, health and safety. Many not-for-profit organizations post PSAs on their websites.

Brochures

There are a number of questions you should ask yourself before developing a brochure:

- What is the main audience?
- How will it be distributed?
- What is the organization's database like? Does it also include email addresses?
- What is the possible budget?
- What is the objective?

When developing a brochure for an organization, the first step is to create a formal plan, which should include the following components:

- Preamble
- Objectives
- Strategic considerations
- Product or organizational backgrounder
- Target audiences and markets
- Three key messages

Once the plan is approved, a story board should be created. When producing the brochure, make sure you design an electronic version as well that can be used as an e-flyer.

Op-Eds

What Is an Op-Ed and When Is It Useful?

"Op-ed" is short for "opposite the editorial page," a concept that originated with the *New York Times*. An op-ed is an article, *not* an essay, which builds to its point. It is an excellent opportunity for individuals and/or organizations to reach an audience of opinion leaders, as well as a great opportunity for an organization's executive to become a spokesperson for a particular industry, cause or issue. (Industry groups, universities, and think tanks are often originators of such pieces).

It is also a way for an organization to get the "real" story out. *The Globe and Mail* and the *National Post* are the main national conduits for op-eds in Canada. But regional or local papers also publish op-eds, such as the *Toronto Star*, *Ottawa Citizen* (a good place for pieces with a political slant or target) or *Calgary Herald* (especially for oil patch issues).

Op-eds can also be published by trade publications covering specific industries.

Tips for Writing and Offering Op-Eds

- Keep it between 400 and 750 words (the length preferred by daily newspapers).
- Present one main idea or single theme.
- Have a clear editorial viewpoint about current social issues, situations or news.
- Get to your point in the first paragraph, then back up your opinion with facts and stats (ratio of opinion to fact should be 20 per cent opinion to 80 per cent fact).
- Use short declarative sentences.
- Avoid "I"; write in the journalistic third person.
- Use active—*not* passive—verbs.
- Describe the writer's background in the cover letter or note.
- Follow standard practice by offering the op-ed to one publication at a time.
- Query editors before sending an op-ed to see if there is interest in the first place.

Letters to the Editor

A letter to the editor is an effective way of refuting or elaborating on previous news coverage and opinion columns. Here are some tips:

- Always check to see whom to send it to and the publication's requirements.
- Keep it short—100 to 200 words or less.
- Be temperate, factual, and unemotional.
- Identify the subject in the opening paragraph.
- Identify the article or editorial, if it's a response, and when and where it was published (sometimes a newspaper loves to publish views taking issue with its competitors).
- State the theme of the letter in the second paragraph (agree, disagree, want clarification on something).
- Give your viewpoint, with back-up facts, in the next several paragraphs.
- Provide your name, title, organization, and telephone number/email address at the end of the letter. Publications often will contact writers of letters for confirmation purposes.

Don't Be a "Time Bandit"

Scott White, a longtime media veteran, advises the public relations community to not be a "time bandit" when it comes to interfacing with extremely busy journalists.

White, former editor-in-chief of the Canadian Press, notes "the primary job for CP is to cover the day's spot news developments, preparing material for a national audience. So what might be appealing to the morning jocks of an FM radio station probably won't be of much interest to CP."

Following up new product stories and pitching to multiple editors within CP not only irritates journalists unnecessarily, but actually steals valuable time from this news operation that runs on minute-to-minute deadlines 24/7. Hence, White's term "time bandit."

"We receive literally hundreds of communications from PR professionals each day," he said. "Some of our editors, especially those in business and health/lifestyles, can barely keep up with the flood of information. What is most maddening from an editor's perspective is a call about something that our organization would have absolutely no interest in covering, such as new product news."

Many of us in the media relations trenches know that getting one of our client's stories covered by The Canadian Press is often the "holy grail" of our "beat." Pick-up by The Canadian Press and the 1,500 news media outlets, print, broadcast, and online, that subscribe to CP literally means at least 10 million impressions when all is said and done.

White's best advice to PR professionals is to "anticipate, anticipate, anticipate. We need to deal with PR people who not only react quickly when we need quick reaction, but actually anticipate that we'll need reaction before the event happens. This works when PR professionals know the day's scheduled news events and can offer up comment or information as quickly as possible."

Monitoring CP wire stories published by daily newspapers and distributed in real time by the CP Command News service will certainly help PR pros understand what CP is interested in and know when clients can add to the steady flow of news from CP's Toronto headquarters and seven bureaus. For busy PR pros, receiving the CP news feed wirelessly is a good way to stay on top of what interests CP and what news it carries, enabling practitioners to react quickly to news developments.

Knowing when to call and pitch is also very important. Former general news director Mike Omelus said he would take calls from PR pros he knew would bring newsworthy information to the table the one or two times a year that they reached out to him. "PR is essential in helping the news media get the job done. It's an important relationship. But knowing our needs, and those of other news organizations, will help you understand what we and other outlets will consider newsworthy."

The Canadian Press is affiliated with the largest news agency in the world, the Associated Press (AP). CP delivers real-time text, audio, photos, graphics and online services to newspapers, broadcasters, publishers, web sites, wireless carriers, cable companies, and even elevator screens and gas station pumps.

Making the Call

When I was a journalist, the inundation of information was mind-boggling. News releases arriving by fax, media kits arriving by courier, newswire stories provided by The Canadian Press, all followed by hundreds of phone calls made by well-intentioned people wanting to know if I had received their information and was interested in their story. Sometimes these calls worked when their news was packaged as a tight sound bite. Sometimes I would scramble and dig into the blue box looking for a kit that seemed interesting after the "verbal sell." But not usually.

And now that email and some social media channels have significantly increased the flow of information into newsrooms and freelancers' home offices, how can one follow-up telephone call cut through all the "noise"? What follows are some suggestions from two journalists in the field.

Marc Saltzman, who is one of North America's most successful freelance technology journalists in both print and broadcast, receives about 300 emails per day, but takes very few calls. He hates the phone. "The phone ruins my writing flow, email is much more conducive," he says.

Which leads to follow-up call tip #1. Find out the journalist's communication preference.

Online media databases and directories (available from services such as Cision) include journalist preferences when it comes to receiving news releases and related information. PR practitioners who subscribe to these types of databases are also able to record their own notes, tips and bits of information on particular journalists or media outlets. Knowing a journalist's preferred means of contact as well as any additional information like deadlines, story preferences, technological savvy, etc., can make the process of media relations simpler and more effective.

Saltzman stresses that practitioners should "choose their battles" for follow-up calls. "Isolate the important stories." He also notes how important it is to do your homework as a PR professional. For example, don't follow up on an inapplicable lifestyle story with a tech product journalist.

John Valorzi, former business editor at The Canadian Press, received about 200 emails and between 75 and 100 telephone calls per day when he was in the job. He liked phone calls, by the way, as long as they were worthwhile and provided context. "I don't mind receiving [follow-up] calls, but more than half are from juniors who simply ask if I got the release, not from seniors who can debate things or tell me the context."

Valorzi points out that two or three times a week he got follow-up calls from practitioners wondering if a release was of interest when it had already moved on The Canadian Press wire three or four hours earlier. Monitor the CP wire before you call!

He also recommends including data that makes a story newsworthy. For example, if a product is being launched, how many jobs will it create? How much money will be spent on building the new plant? *That* is worthwhile follow-up information that *will* interest journalists like him.

And he reminds us to do post-mortems on stories that bomb out. "Did it have hard edge, quantifiable information that lifted the release beyond just a product release? Before being called 100 times, the PR person has to understand that content is king."

How to Make Your Video Work

For decades television news has been among the most powerful and trusted news media. To get a softer story onto a TV newscast you must follow one paramount rule—*have moving pictures.*

In congested news markets such as Toronto, getting a videographer or camera assigned to your story is a challenge to say the least. If you're lucky, you may get one or two cameras out to your news event. That leaves another three or four stations (not including the networks) that will not cover your story because they are not there with a camera.

PR practitioners can maximize their TV impact by investing in video and hiring a news videography service.

Tips for Video

- Hire a videographer with news experience (and union credentials)—wedding video won't cut it!
- Shoot it in high definition.
- Footage should be edited, eye-catching, and delivered in a timely manner.
- Don't shoot shots—shoot sequences. Tell the story.
- Produce a shot list to use as a rough guide.
- Allow for time to light the shot properly.
- Shoot as a news videographer would shoot it—don't make it too polished.
- Keep the video visually entertaining.
- Work with the camera operator/producer to capture the best shots and sequences.
- Hire a staging company when it is a news event so that lighting, backdrop signage and audio feeds are all present and in working order.

Distribution of video is dependent on budget and timing. If it is a relatively hard news story with time sensitivities, courier delivery of the tapes if it's a one-market focus, satellite delivery if it's of national interest, and/or the use of Internet download services such as Hightail will be necessary.

Ensure concise, hard-copy news materials accompany the video and make sure the video clip is not too long—under ten minutes is ideal. TV stations don't have the time or staff to go through long tapes! Check on submission requirements because many TV newsrooms are fully digital.

These tips also hold true for web video, which is in high demand these days as print media market their online editions and utilize web video on those sites. The Internet is becoming a "broadcast medium," with moving pictures, as opposed to its tradition of being a print medium, with text and still images. Two service providers for web video are The Canadian Press Images and News Canada.

How to Make Your PR Photos Work

One of the most effective tools for getting positive news coverage is the still photograph.

Whether aimed at community newspapers or the larger dailies, PR photos that get picked up by publications can powerfully convey your organization's message. But there is a real art and science to the news photo.

Ron Welch is general manager of The Canadian Press Images, a division of CP. Welch says "editors know the value of good pictures—they draw readers' attention, they sell papers and they can make or break your chances of getting your point across."

Welch, who has been in the photo business for 30 years, offers 10 tips to help communicators get the best out of their news photo.

Ron Welch's 10 Tips for Effective PR Photos

1. Hire a photographer with editorial experience. They understand what photo editors are looking for and will deliver images in the correct digital format, colour corrected and ready to go.
2. Good photos are novel and in some way unusual.
3. A good photo shows action the instant it happens.
4. Strong photos portray people and appeal to the emotions.
5. They always relate to some important person, event or place.
6. The photo should wrap up a story and provide an overall view of it.
7. Remember context—excellent news photos tie in with a current story, the season, the weather, a fad.
8. Large empty spaces should always be avoided in news photos. The entire frame should contain useful information.
9. Stand-up group shots, unless filled with VIPs, don't work.
10. The digital format of choice is an 8X10, 300 dpi JPEG.

PR photos can be distributed in a number of ways, including through paid wire services such as Cision and the CP itself and directly to photo editors via email. The latter distribution tactic should not be overlooked, because some community newspapers and smaller dailies do not subscribe to paid wire services, and they tend to be heavy users of photos generated by PR, especially of local events or people. Keep captions under 50 words!

Media Events: Maximizing Your Attendance and News Pick-up

As the news media become more saturated with information, particularly in news hotspots such as Toronto or Montreal, journalists find it increasingly difficult to attend media events.

Here's why.

Electronic highways into newsrooms have enabled a shrinking newsroom workforce to cover more territory because of the concentration of information into databases and the plethora of internal and external wire services. The widespread adoption of email increases information flow. Working on very short deadlines, most journalists are reluctant to leave their desks for a story.

As we noted earlier, research firm Ipsos Reid found in 2005 that business journalists received about 150 news releases per week, of which only about 18 per cent were used. As you can imagine, the flood of incoming information has only increased since then.

Your task, as a media relations practitioner, is to make your story as easy to digest as possible and readily accessible via electronic communications. When your story is highly visual through the presence of celebrity spokespersons or a particular location or geography, plan your event with the following considerations in mind:

- Find out what is going on before picking the date and time—pay attention to the news and advanced notification of events. The Canadian Press provides online access to its calendar of events viewed by daily newspapers.
- Make it downtown, as close to news media outlets as you can.
- Make it late morning or early afternoon to enable media to get there on their rounds after their morning story meetings and before late afternoon deadlines.

Capitalize on the Visuals by Hiring Your Own Photographer and/or Videographer

Hiring a photographer/videographer enables you to provide media-ready images to news outlets or post them online for access by journalists who are unable to attend your event. Having your own images also permits you to document the event in your own fashion and provides a permanent archival record for future reference. Your organization also owns the work! Hire someone already trusted by the news media, perhaps a freelancer who works for a wire service or news organization. For example, The Canadian Press's Images division, which I've already mentioned, specializes in capturing "news-style" photos that the news media want. Services provided by well-known and trusted companies such as CP Photo Assignment Services can either be the ultimate insurance policy in case only a few media representatives show up (or even none at all), or can serve to expand an event's media coverage.

The need for speed is paramount. You should have the final photography and videography into news media hands by 3:30 p.m. or 4 p.m. at the latest. Let them know by voice and email that it's coming. At the event itself, try to engineer a great shot. Trust the news photographer you have hired—they know their business. Move the chosen photo on a paid wire service. Write a tight, newsworthy caption. Have an electronic version ready to email to media on demand as well as posting it at a specific URL for easy, self-serve downloading.

Have high-resolution video shot and, if you have the budget and time, edit it properly and get it into the media's hands by the 4 p.m. deadline. Have hard copy accompany it, and, ideally, a USB containing the whole news kit in electronic form. Make sure you have good clips of all the spokespeople involved, capture the ambiance of the event, include wild (or natural) sound and make the video short—less than 10 minutes.

News events also offer another important aspect beyond generating news coverage. You can create events that include customers and/or employees. And there is always the intangible effect of a successful news event. It raises morale within a company. There's nothing more exciting for employees than to see their company featured in the news in a positive light. And good news can go a long way in helping the HR folks to promote a healthy work environment.

Create a Media Section on Your Web Site

Web site media sections are an opportunity for an organization to provide the news media with an easy-to-use, multimedia platform to disseminate information about that organization and its news.

A web site "newsroom," a term that seems to be gaining acceptance in mainstream usage, should contain that information in at least two easy-to-download formats, Word and PDFs. The news media have little time as it is, and do *not* have the time to spend digging for information, cutting-and-pasting or reformatting information that they intend to use in a story.

"Often when we are on deadline, we have space to fill and need these materials faster than PR contacts can deliver," says Gordon Brockhouse, former editor-in-chief of *Here's How* magazine. "This often happens after normal business hours. The company that makes it easiest for us, by having information and images available online, is the one that gets the space."

The web site newsroom should at the very least also contain high-resolution (8X10, 300 dpi) photography. MP3s are another information source, primarily for radio news consumption, that are easy to capture and inexpensively park in the web site newsroom.

Don't forget that web video is also a good educative tool. "I wouldn't be likely to use video myself, but I often go to a web site to find out about things, using the video archive," says food writer and editor Liz Campbell. "I find I learn more quickly with auditory and visual input than by reading."

Campbell also notes that the media section should be easy to find on the web site. The newsroom link button should be prominently displayed, such as on the far left side of the web page, the same position that journalists are trained to regard as holding the most important information on a printed page.

Content of the newsroom should not only be in multimedia format, easy-to-download text, still images and video, but should also be brief in nature, a series of fact sheets and quotations. Longer pieces can also be parked there, such as white papers, speeches, and annual reports. Over time, a significant archive can be built.

Lots of time and money are spent on web site design, but a survey of web site media sections shows that the media section is not given enough attention.

Journalists need 24/7 access to web site newsrooms so passwording the section can be problematic unless that function works very quickly and seamlessly. While understanding that this tactic helps with the media monitoring process, many journalists surveyed do not like it, and find the process obtrusive and time consuming. Nothing but public information should be parked in a web site newsroom anyway, so passwording may be counterproductive.

Media Relations Measurement Paradigm Levels Playing Field

Evaluation of media coverage has always been a problem. Credibility was always at the mercy of the many different paradigms used to calculate reach and quality.

After four years in development under the leadership of Tracey Bochner, her group of senior agency, industry and client side media relations specialists launched the Media Relations Ratings Points (MRP) system, now called Media Rating Points to include PESO, in partnership with the Canadian Public Relations Society (CPRS).

To understand how valuable this media relations measurement paradigm is, look at how media relations evaluation was conducted previously.

Generally, it starts with audience numbers. MRP subscribes to several services to get third-party audited audience reach data for print, web, blogs radio and TV. "For broadcast, if you called an outlet and asked different people who work there on both the editorial and sales sides, you would probably get different answers on the 'reach' because those numbers depend on how that department reports the numbers, which could be total show reach, quarter-hour audience reach or even total station reach," Bochner observes.

MRP, by contrast, provides consistency. The system uses standardized data on print readership via Vividata, and provides data from media planners for broadcast that are often inaccessible to PR firms unless they have official advertising agency status or ad agency partners. The cost for the data is modest (and there is a discount for CPRS members).

All of the audience data, including web site audience information (from ComScore), is provided by Fifth Story, which won the RFP. "We're delighted to be working on this project and believe it is very important to clients to have a common media relations measurement paradigm," says Ruth Douglas, former CEO of Fifth Story.

What MRP does not do is provide advertising equivalencies, and rightfully so. That form of measurement poses several problems. Firstly, editorial cannot be purchased and therefore cannot have an advertising equivalency. As Bochner puts it: "You simply cannot buy media coverage!" Secondly, editorial often has far more third-party word-of-mouth generation power than does advertising. Bochner adds: "You can't buy space on the front page, above the fold, so how would you measure that through ad equivalencies? It doesn't make any sense."

In a nutshell, the MRP system provides a score based on standardized criteria that incorporate tone as well. The tone plus the ratings generate an overall percentage score. "In the tests we have done to date with our clients, we consider 75 per cent or above a good campaign," says Bochner. The system also works out a cost per contact (this is where the standardized reach data becomes useful), "so our clients can demonstrate ROI to their stakeholders and evaluate a program's success compared to other campaigns," notes Bochner.

A Proverbial Needle in an Electronic Haystack

A combination of revisions to the Canadian copyright law and the trend towards subscription-based news media web sites (and subsequent silos hidden from web search engines and other media monitoring services) has made the media monitoring task feel at times like a search for a needle in an electronic haystack.

"With copyright licensing and high technology investment, media monitoring definitely has gotten more expensive," says John Weinseis, former president, Bowdens Media Monitoring Ltd. (now Cision). "But the results have also improved dramatically in terms of speed and quality. New services have been developed by many participants to provide multi-media portal based delivery along with rudimentary analysis. The bigger concern seems to be the ability to weed out irrelevant material."

One very senior and savvy Toronto-based practitioner uses at least seven different services to provide her clients with accurate and timely media monitoring reports. Media monitoring services have been hindered by these new regulatory and competitive realities, while at least one senior independent media relations practitioner thinks of throwing in the towel some days because the media monitoring task has become so expensive and time consuming.

Agencies that have a number of junior practitioners on staff definitely have a competitive advantage these days since they can afford the extremely time-consuming deep web searches, conduct the old-fashioned read-and-clip services themselves, and chase hard-copy and electronic media coverage once they know it has been published or broadcast.

How do we survive this media monitoring nightmare?

- Subscribe to as many media monitoring services as budget permits and lobby hard to get a large enough budget to do a good job.
- Train in-house staff and clients to accurately seek and report coverage as a team effort.
- Build in inherent tracking systems for media follow-up to chase as much coverage as possible.
- Get on as many comp lists as you can.
- Subscribe to all key media within the client's category.
- Deliberately build in key words and specifically named quotes in news releases to help with electronic monitoring.
- Hire as many web savvy under-25's as possible.

- Beg every journalist who has promised coverage to send you tear sheets, MP3s, MP4s, and DVDs, give them your courier account numbers to send them at no charge, and send profuse thank-you's afterwards.

Correcting Misinformation

Often, demanding a correction or apology will bring attention to misinformation that readers may have missed in the first place, causing more harm than good.

So be sure it really is important to correct misinformation. Misquotations are often not worth fixing if the only problem is they weren't verbatim. If the product's price is only off a few dollars, why bother the reporter who rounded it off?

However, if there is a blatant factual error, work with the reporter directly to have it corrected in the media outlet's database. (If you can't get it fixed that way, then go to that reporter/columnist's editor next. Don't jump over anyone's head as a knee-jerk reaction.)

Information can spread far and wide so you want the error fixed at the source. But only do so if it is really important! Don't demand a correction notice that will likely get buried on page 150. But do ensure the public record is correct.

Social Media: Are You a Cybersaur?

Cybersaur is a term I officially coined in the *Toronto Star* in 2010. It means, tongue-in-cheek, those who communicate only by email.

I am constantly asked while developing speaking notes and lectures to address media relations and social media.

First of all, they are two separate disciplines. Since the jury is still out on whether or not the public relations function will end up responsible for social media, or if it will fall into the hands of broader marketing communicators such as advertising agencies, or carve out its own niche all together, within or outside customer service departments, it is not included in the graphic on page 3.

There are other semantic considerations here as well.

First of all, many media relations professionals have been practising social media tactics for years if the definition is broad and includes web video, audio, interactive web pages, and web-based newsrooms.

And many actually communicate with journalists via social media channels such as Twitter, Facebook and LinkedIn.

But most media members I have informally canvassed still like getting news from us via email.

Most certainly, the social media phenomenon is eating away a journalist's most valuable commodity, *time*. Many are now spending several hours a day communicating with their audiences via social media. So adding this channel to our mix of getting information to the media, on top of email, paid newswire, regular mail and of course, telephone calls, may not be the best idea. However, as previously counselled in this book, find out what your media targets want, and how they want to receive it!

There has been a vast migration of advertising dollars from traditional media (print, broadcast and electronic versions thereof) to social media.

There has also been a crackdown on "blogola," paying for positive treatment in various blogs or elsewhere. Ethically, this poses immense issues for PR practitioners. In a nutshell, if a "paid" endorsement of a product or service is not obvious, by prominently displaying the label "sponsored content" or another such descriptor, it is considered unethical, and actually illegal in Canada and some other jurisdictions. Make sure you're familiar with the CPRS Code of Professional Standards, which can be found on the CPRS web site, and which states: "Members shall personally accept no fees, commissions, gifts or any other considerations for professional services from anyone except employers or clients for whom the services were specifically performed" (www.cprs.ca).

Always Build Two Benches with the Same Wood

A final note on strategy.

Often practicing PR is akin to building puzzles. It's left to us to proactively, gently, and, many times, almost invisibly blend an organization's opportunities and problems into a delectable morsel for one or more of our organization's publics.

PR is not rocket science. It's not science at all. In fact, it's far more art than science because it's very intuitive. However, intuition is very difficult to sell. It's a great starting point, but you will need formal strategic structure to not only "sell" the program or campaign, but to get key messaging through the gatekeepers, including the news media.

In order for PR to work, it must be very strategic and it is in many ways the most strategic of all the marketing communications disciplines. One of the fundamentals of effective modern PR practice is research. Research can particularly identify a program or campaign's target audience, an underpinning of strategy—an absolutely crucial one. Or, if you will allow the metaphor, the frame to be used in building your bench—the strategic framework for all marketing communications.

Practitioners can then create planks for that bench for each marketing communications discipline such as public relations (of course), promotions, sponsorships, advertising, and web site and other electronic communications. The power of integrated communications can then be realized. Your target audience has a common place to sit and absorb the messaging.

This is what I call "building two benches with the same wood." As a hobby, I have built benches. And when the weather permits, I sit on them to think about my clients and students and how I can constantly improve what I do and how I do it. I call this "bench time."

This metaphor can also be applied tactically, especially in the ever recurring times of budget restraint. Practitioners can look for opportunities to blend a number of tactics to meet common objectives—for example, launching three products together instead of one, or satisfying both external and internal communications objectives at the same time.

Finally, "building two benches with the same wood" is a great replacement for the old saying that involves harming small birds!

Acknowledgements

There are many people to thank for not just this edition with Centennial Press—kudos to David Stover and Dean Nate Horowitz—but also the many who were involved in both the first and second editions as well. I am very grateful to Centennial Press for helping to get this book to third edition, and to be part of such of a progressive press.

First and foremost is Bill Carney, who met me when this book was at first draft and encouraged me to get it out there. I wrote it as a companion to his stalwart *In The News*, of which I find myself a co-author in its third edition (University of Alberta Press). Bill also enabled me to have a chapter in his *Fundamentals of Public Relations and Marketing Communications* (also University of Alberta Press). He has been a mentor for many years and has graciously provided a foreword for this edition.

Secondly, Daniel Granger was an early peer reviewer and has supported this book and my career for many years. He is only the fourth professional communicator in Canada's history to be appointed to the Order of Canada. It has indeed been an honour to have had his support and friendship all these years.

Thirdly, many clients allowed me to use our case studies in this book. And every client always teaches me something, some more than others, and for that learning I am always grateful. Thank you to Bryan Asa, Scott Bierwiler, Knut Brundtland, Janet Culliton, Peter Joe, Kevin Kelly, SJ, David Prosser, Barry Richler, Erik Sorensen, SJ, and Filomena Williams.

Many of my public relations, journalism, design, legal and accounting colleagues and friends have also helped immensely, namely Colin Babiuk, Ira Basen, Patrick Blake, Tracey Bochner, Gordon Brockhouse, Jennifer Cruxton, Karen Dalton, Ruth Douglas, the late Steve Dekter, Anne Galt, Richard Harlow, Todd LaVigne, Christina Marshall, Dom Mastropietro, Larry O'Donoghue, Mike Omelus, Derrick Pieters, Ian Ross, Marc Saltzman, John Valorzi, Ron Welch, John Weinseis, and Scott White.

Lastly, to my students of many years in both the academic and corporate environments, many of whom have supported this book with positive comments that keep those of us in the PR wilderness going sometimes! This book is for you, along with our growing Canadian body of PR knowledge, to enable our next generations of PR practitioners to do better than we did, something which is imperative to maintain this wonderful democracy we call Canada.

Mark Hunter LaVigne
Aurora, Ontario
2019

About the Author

Mark Hunter LaVigne, MA, APR, FCPRS, knows both sides of the "media fence" well. For five years prior to his career in media relations, he was a national on-air radio journalist and since 1990, he has worked in public relations agencies including his own media relations and media training practice.

After completing a Master of Arts in Journalism at the University of Western Ontario's Graduate School of Journalism, Mark worked as a radio journalist in Calgary, Edmonton, and Toronto. Prior to UWO, he completed an Honours Bachelor of Arts in Mass Communications and English at York University in Toronto. He went to a Jesuit high school prior to that, also located in Toronto.

He is an award-winning, accredited member (APR) of the Canadian Public Relations Society (CPRS), a member of the College of Fellows (FCPRS), is a Past-President of CPRS (Toronto) and past Vice-President on the national CPRS board.

His awards include CPRS Toronto ACE awards for Crossled, Pete's Tofu and the Canadian Canoe Pilgrimage, and a national CPRS Award of Excellence for the Canadian Canoe Pilgrimage.

He regularly speaks at conferences and workshops and guest lectures, and has taught in PR programs at Ryerson University, Western University, Seneca at York, Centennial College, and Humber College.

His hobbies include playing guitar and harmonica, song writing, recording and performing both, photography, canoe tripping and backpacking in his beloved Algonquin Park, and working with wood, building benches and other patio furniture, as well as assembling (so far) one guitar.

A father of four, he has lived in Aurora, Ontario for many years.

www.ingramcontent.com/pod-product-compliance
Lightning Source LLC
Chambersburg PA
CBHW071658210326
41597CB00017B/2242